To Frankl

You are special. An amazing person. Keep demonstrating greater achievements.

ERNEST MOSES

Young Achievers

How To Become The Achiever
You Were Born To Be

REVISED AND EXPANDED EDITION

This book was first published with the:
ISBN: 978-0-9575580 ISBN – 13: 978-0-9575580-0-7

Revised and Expanded Edition:
ISBN: 978-0-9575580 ISBN – 13: 978-0-9575580-1-4

Email us at info@youngachieversgroup.com
Visit our website at www.youngachieversgroup.com
Find out more about this book at www.books.youngachieversgroup.com

Everything you want is inside you.
Live from the inside out.

Dedication

To the human heart.

To all who seek fulfilment in their lives to
become the Achievers, they were born to be.

To Young People in this generation and the
generations to come. May you discover yourselves
and advance towards a worthwhile goal.

To my two daughters,
Trishna Shalom and Sianna-Divine.
May you become the Achievers
you were born to be.

To everyone who seeks to be an Achiever.
May you discover the Achiever in you.

Acknowledgement

My gratitude to all, both young and old, who have taught me. I am forever grateful for your inspiration and wisdom. You have taught me how to live my life from the inside out; your thoughts, words and ideas have truly seasoned me for this moment in time. As we are a sum of what we have learned from those who taught us, to mention but a few, I would like to say thank you to:

Dr Mensa Otabil, the General Overseer of International Central Gospel Church, for your living words that continue to inspire me.

Reverend Donkor for your shepherding arm and fatherliness.

All of the inspirational teachers and leaders in my life.

My wonderful King's Temple family for your encouraging words and steadfast support.

The network of young people that I have had the privilege of serving throughout the years through Young King's (YKC) and the Young Achievers Group (YAG). For every Young Achiever around the world, this book was written because of you.

My formidable team of Youth Facilitators, I want to thank you for your continued support and love.

Let me express my profound appreciation to those who have supported me from the conception and publication of this book:

My dear wife, Alberta and our daughters, Trishna Shalom and Sianna-Divine. Thank you for your unyielding passion, support and patience during the production of this book. You make it easier for me to fulfil the purpose of my life.

My parents, Moses and Agarthar, and all my siblings: your constant demonstrations of love have inspired me to pursue my purpose in life.

Chanika, our YAG Director: as well as being a committed personal assistant throughout the production of this work, you are indeed an integral part of this vision. The world awaits your greatness.

Brenda of Taygo Bren. Thank you for your partnership all these years, specifically the beautiful book cover design, unapparelled ideas and perspectives.

Ruth. Thank you for proofreading the manuscript and making those unique suggestions.

Nathalie. Thank you for reviewing the manuscript and working with me to refine it.

Last but not least, to Kevin, thank you for working with me to edit this book. Thank you all.

Contents

Introduction

Derrick was outside late one afternoon, busy searching for something. As he searched thoroughly and in desperation, his older brother, James, was walking by.

"Derrick, are you okay?"

"Does it look like I'm okay?" Derrick replied.

"What's wrong?" James asked in a caring tone.

"I can't find my car keys, and I'm looking for them," he said with so much frustration in his voice.

The young man joined in the search for the keys, and after searching fruitlessly for a while, he turned to his brother and asked, "Derrick, do you at least remember where you might have left them?"

Derrick took some time. "The last place was in the house," he said sheepishly. "That's where I last saw them."

James got angry. "Why are you then out here looking for the keys when you know that you left them inside the house!"

This apologue is a reflection of the human experience. Many people are busy searching externally for things that they already have inside of them. This is mission impossible. It is on this basis that this book is written, suggesting to you a profound truth and principle – only when you live from the inside out, do you reign in life.

In *"If It Ain't Broke...Break It"*, authors Robert J. Kriegel and Louis Patler cite a study of 1,500 people over a twenty-year period that points to this principle of living from the inside out. In their study, Kriegel and Patler establish how doing things you are passionate about or working with your talent, can make a significant difference in your career. The group was divided into Groups A and B. Group A comprised 83% of the sample, who were pursuing a career to fund their future endeavours. Group B, the other 17% of the sample, were pursuing their passion and desired financial benefits later in life. At the end of the twenty-year period of the study, 101 of the 1,500 participants had become millionaires. Of the 101 millionaires, 100 were from the group that had chosen to pursue what they loved first, Group B.

There is a popular phrase that says, *"Find something you like to do so much that you'd gladly do it for nothing, and if you learn to do it well, someday people will be happy to pay you for it."* There is really no substitute for passion when it comes to work. You must discover something you really enjoy and then do it. Steve Jobs stated that *"Your work is going to fill a large part of your life, and the only way to be truly satisfied is to do what you believe is great work. And the only way to do great work is to love what you do. If you haven't found it yet, keep looking. Don't settle. As with all matters of the heart, you'll know when you find it."*

This book is an instruction manual to help you to live from the inside out. To transform your outer reality, you must inwardly achieve what you want to see on the outside. This is a model for all achievements in life; before anything is seen on the outside, it must first be achieved on the inside. Before anything is created on the outside, it first must be created on the inside. Let's say you want to improve your grades in school. You must first create a mental picture of the grades you desire and hold unto it until it becomes your reality. This life principle enables you to create the life you desire. You are therefore responsible for your progress in life. By understanding, observing and applying this principle, you guarantee your success in life. In essence, it is not where you are in life on the outside that counts; it is where you are on the inside.

But of course, we cannot discuss the principle of living from the inside out, without acknowledging the urgency and importance of discovering your authentic self. Discovering who you are is essential to your fulfilment in life. All over the world, people remain confused about their identity, leading to most of the stress or frustration-related ailments of today. Clinical Psychologist Dr Edward A. Dreyfus deconstructs this point in his book, 'Living Life from the Inside Out'. He explains that, *"Using a false-self causes stress and all kinds of other psychological issues. One of the roads to psychological health is to live authentically, decreasing our false-self and increasing living as our real-selves."*

Simply put, people are not living their true selves, and this is the plight of millions of people. We yearn to know the purpose of our existence. A simple search on the Internet on, 'What is my purpose?' or 'Who am I?', elicits billions of results. Every single person possesses an innate yearning to understand the purpose of their existence. In search of this absolute truth, people are willing to travel to 'distant lands' and foreign spaces, instead of looking at their own 'backyard', right 'inside' of them.

I hope that this book will help you receive a glimpse of the purpose of your life as you discover yourself through its pages. Young Achievers brings out the idea that what you are looking for on the outside is within you. All over the world, people are in search of one thing or the other, and the most important place these things can be found is inside of them. Inside of each person, lies the answer to every question and the solution to every problem. You are the solution to the world's problems.

When we come to the point of possessing absolute knowledge of what is in us, it will always put us on the **Path of Achievers**. These truths have been attested by great thinkers, including Socrates, who once said: *"An unexamined life is not worth living."* We must be willing to self-examine to gain self-knowledge on our unique abilities and individual potentialities, which in turn will help us to be effective on Earth.

In this book, you will discover that the power to be what you want to be, to get what you desire, to accomplish whatever you are striving for, is within you. You have potentialities and abilities, which, when properly grasped and directed, can lift you out of the channel of mediocrity and enable you to fulfil your destiny. For example, you can become a lawyer, writer, statesman, entrepreneur or whatever your life's aim is, or destiny is.

To achieve this, you will need to discover this treasure in you. You will need to appreciate the unique qualities and strength you have inside of you. Additionally, this book will give you the tools to discover who you truly are and stir you up for greatness, and help you live a life of achievements.

This book is for the youth, but it is recommended to everyone who desires to discover their purpose. The thoughts in this book are based on life principles and can be applied by everyone who desires to make a difference in the world as they work to fulfil their destiny. The true definition of youth is a state of mind as described by R. Kennedy: *"This world demands the qualities of youth: not a time of life but a state of mind, a temper of the will, a quality of imagination, a predominance of courage over timidity, of the appetite for adventure over the life of ease."*

As we embark on this journey, I urge you to have an open mind and be ready to engage with the principles, strategies and techniques outlined here. If you practise them, it does not matter where you are in life or what has happened to you; you will begin to make progress in your life. It is said that procrastination is the cause of failure in the life of most people. Most times, the knowledge we acquire falls short because we fail to put it into practise. Therefore, you must discover your potential and act now. In the words of Lao Tzu: *"A journey of a thousand miles begins with a single step."* You must make up your mind today that you are going to unleash your potential to make a difference in your world.

My desire is that you will take these timeless principles into your life and live by them. Do this, and I know you will become the achiever you were born to be.

CHAPTER ONE

The Path of Achievers

O ne evening, after a meeting with my team about a workshop we were planning to run, I received a call from one of the young people in our organisation. His panicked voice was enough to raise an alarm. He was facing expulsion from his university due to non-attendance and other misdemeanours. The news struck me. He said to me, "Ernest, I've found myself on the wrong path, can you help me, please?" This incident and many similar issues affecting the lives of young people are the reasons why I now run a range of workshops, webinars and coaching and mentoring programs to empower young people to take the path of an achiever.

Understanding the Path of Achievers

The Path of Achievers is the roadmap needed to become an achiever. Most of us desire to be achievers in life but not every person feels like they can. This is because many people live their lives from the *outside* in instead of from the *inside out.* In other words, they depend on external factors or variables to define them instead of finding an innate reason for living. One of the most profound human needs is to be significant. The yearning for significance and relevance is what drives people to get out of bed every morning to do what they believe is important for their lives. This need suggests that there is an internal void in the human soul of which, I propose to you, is filled by the pursuit of purpose.

While watching the news recently, I saw a young man being questioned by the authorities to find out why he had committed a crime. He confessed he wanted to gain notoriety. In like manner, the need to be significant in the eyes of others can drive people to take drastic actions.

From a positive lens, success and influence do not just fall into our laps. There are things we need to do and engage with to get those results. If you look through history, people who attained significance and achieved meaningful outcomes did so by abiding by certain fundamental principles and habits. In essence, there are underlying principles that we must develop or integrate into our character that will form the foundation of our achievements on Earth. This is the path all achievers take to meet their need for significance.

The Path of Achievers represents the right path in life that avoids any path that can lead you into negative terrain, bringing painful and regrettable results. It is important to note that there is also a wrong path. For example, in the United Kingdom, knife crime has become a cancer in our society. There are young people taking paths which are leading to their deaths and the deaths of other young people. We all have a choice to make—we can choose the Path of Achievers, or choose the wrong path. I suggest you choose the Path of Achievers so that you may live and meaningfully contribute to society. In the words of David Starr Jordan, *"There is no real excellence in all this world which can be separated from right living."*

Criteria for Recognising the Right Path

There are three criteria to determine you are on the right path.

1. Societal ethics - the right path makes you a good citizen of society.
2. Purpose - the right path brings about a sense of direction that you are on your way towards a definite destination.
3. Useful - the right path brings you great value along the way. A useful path makes the journey fruitful.

When you see these three elements on your path, it suggests you are on the Path of Achievers.

Finding Your Path

On the journey of life, we do not all have the same path. Our paths are unique to our destination. You need to find and understand your unique path.

We all make our own decisions, and these decisions create our future. Every twist, turn, and miraculous detour has its purpose. To discover your distinctive path in life, start by appreciating your unique tendencies and listening to your inner promptings. Finding your path is akin to discovering your purpose.

Remember, every destination in life requires a path or route. If you are travelling from one city to another city, it will require a path, route or road to get there. The same principle applies to reaching the highest level of achievement in life, and becoming the achiever you were born to be. Choosing your path could lead you to a certain career, vocation, leadership and other areas of your life.

Throughout time, people who led purpose-driven lives succeeded in getting to their destinations. This made their lives less stressful, and more effective, efficient and fulfilling.

Sometimes in life, when we see people who have done great things, we admire them and seek to emulate them and as a result, sometimes idolise them. Some people are so committed to their 'idols' they buy their branded products, crashing websites and selling out products in minutes, or use their idol's images as screensavers on their laptops and on their phones so they can always be seen. A young woman once told me she has a picture of her 'idol' and talks to the picture every day.

Sunday, November 10, 2019: The Independent
A stampede at Travis Scott's Astroworld music festival in Houston on Saturday left three people hospitalised with leg injuries. Fans began climbing over metal barricades outside the entrance to the event minutes before the gates were scheduled to open at midday. More than 50,000 people were expected to attend.

Stories like this are common on media platforms. People are drawn to achievers in life. Deep inside every one of us possesses a seed of greatness and achievement, so when we see someone living the way we desire to live, we are drawn to them like a moth to a flame.

Sometimes we forget that those ahead of us, who have achieved greatness, first developed a blueprint for greatness in their lives before demonstrating it on the outside. As a youth coach, I have observed that a lot of people in our organisation are passionate about their 'idols' or 'stars' and because of that, they feel connected to them, though they have not met them or know them personally. I do not have anything against having 'idols' or 'stars', but it will be best for us to get to know the real reason that we feel drawn to them. This will help us pursue our calling in life and awaken the sleeping giant within us.

I believe deep inside every one of us lies a power that, if properly understood and harnessed, can enable you to become the person you were born to be. This is called living from the inside out. We have to realise that all the people who found their place in time and fulfilled their destiny, did so with that great ability which lies inside them; from the great businessman to the clergyman, from the scientist to the mathematician, from the athlete to the politician, and many others. They accomplished all those great feats when they discovered themselves and lived from the inside out.

Achievers, I believe, are people who have discovered themselves and are advancing towards a worthwhile goal. Everything you will ever want is inside you. You have been endowed with exceptional abilities and potential, which, if properly understood and nurtured, will make you do great things in life.

Let's take a moment to recollect a great achievement. Thomas Edison invented the light bulb. Yet, his unquenchable hunger to succeed led to 1,000 unsuccessful attempts at inventing the light bulb. I call Edison an achiever because he lived from the inside out and gave birth to something that the world needed. There are so many examples of people who unleashed their talent and potential to promote the welfare of mankind. Until we discover our true self, we might be limited in what we can do. The process of self-discovery begins when we realise our indwelling and unused power. *This sets the beginning and end of our course* — the Path of Achievers.

WHO IS AN ACHIEVER?

As you might have noticed, the Path of Achievers requires a fair amount of responsibility from you to reach your destination. As you engage with the ideas in this book, you will manifest the achiever that you were born to be. There are several definitions of who an achiever is.

According to Collins Dictionary, *a high achiever is someone who is successful in their studies or their work, usually as a result of their efforts.*

Merriam-Webster's Dictionary describes an achiever as *someone who is successful because they are determined and work hard.*

This book describes an achiever as someone who has discovered themselves and is advancing towards a worthwhile goal.

Once an achiever discovers their purpose, this can lead to many benefits including fulfilment, impact, excellent health, wealth, fame, pedigree, followers, ethical business and many more. Whatever we see on the outside is a reflection of what is on the inside. Before the achievements showed on the outside, there was an inward achievement. As I mentioned before, what we achieve inwardly transforms our outer reality.

Qualities of Young Achievers

Throughout history, phenomenal achievers share common attributes that make them who they are. To receive our prize in life, we must develop these qualities to help us work towards becoming the achievers we were born to be. By developing these qualities and making them an integral part of our lives, they will be helpful to us on our path in life.

These qualities are vision, resilience, courage, passion, action, responsibility, creativity, learning, problem-solving and luminary.

Vision

A visionary is someone that can envision the future quickly, marked by foresight, imagination, and wisdom. This quality enables you to create a mental picture of what you want to achieve and a strategy to attain it. Visionaries see the world as to how it ought to be, not how it appears, which promotes the progress of humanity and the world.

Resilience

Resilience is the ability to recover quickly or adjust easily to misfortune, challenges or changes. Resilience requires the subject to adapt to new environments. A resilient person can be likened to an elastic rubber, which bounces back into shape when stretched. This is a quality needed in modern times where things are ever-changing, and the demand to be resilient in the face of adversities should not be underestimated.

Courage

Courage is defined as mental or moral strength to fearlessly venture, persevere, and withstand danger, pain, or difficulty, etc. You must realise that anything worth doing in this life requires courage. If you observe society, you will notice that people who have arrived at their destination in life have stepped out with courage to achieve their goals in life.

Passion

Passion is the energy that drives human effort. It is our intense devotion to someone or something, which drives us beyond what might be considered reasonable behaviour. It is an intense or overmastering feeling or conviction. It is living a life of zest and enthusiasm for something you want. Achievers are passionate about life and about making a difference in the world. They are wholly devoted to a good cause and follow through to the end. This quality is so important because that is what will drive you to persist in the face of adversity and opposition. It will be your fuel to successfully get to your destination.

Action

Pablo Picasso said that *"action is the foundational key to all success."* Goals without action are just dreams. Action is an intentional, conscious measure taken to achieve a goal. For example, things like running or throwing a ball is a function of action. It involves intention, a goal, and a bodily movement guided by the agent. It suggests something done or performed. Action is what propels you to turn your dreams into reality.

Responsibility

Responsibility is the obligation to do something, or have control over or care for someone, as part of one's job or role. This is an attribute that draws ownership out of you, for your life and actions. Achievers take responsibility for their actions and events in their life, taking ownership and making a positive difference in the process.

Creativity

Creativity involves the use of the imagination to design original or unusual ideas to produce something. A creative person can invent and develop innovative ideas across any industry. Achievers exhibit this quality of creativity, which helps them to not only bring new things into the world but also create the life they want.

Learning

Achievers have a learning heart. They have the desire to learn a skill or acquire knowledge in an area of interest by studying, experiencing, or being taught. This quality helps them consistently improve themselves in life, which better positions them to manifest more significant successes in their lives. Lifelong learning is a culture that you should build if you want to maximise your potential in life fully.

Problem Solving

Achievers are problem solvers. They ask questions such as: 'Why are things the way they are in the world? Why is there so much trouble and problems in the world? Why does it look like the issues in the world cannot be dealt with or solved permanently?' These are the contemplations of an achiever. While others are content to just ask "Why?", achievers see problems as opportunities to birth solutions when others are still grumbling about the existing problems. Achievers focus on the problem at hand and integrate information and knowledge to achieve a solution.

Luminary

A luminary is someone who inspires or influences others in a specific field. This person has attained eminence in their field or is an inspiration to others. We are all witnesses to a new generation lighting the Earth with their presence and doing extraordinary and uncommon things. They are luminaries – light-bearers – illuminating the world around them. They are energetic, purposeful and passionate. They are transformers and not conformers. They believe in making a difference and leaving the world a better place than they found it.

REFLECTION

CHAPTER TWO

Be an Achiever

We all have the potential to become achievers. We have in us the inbuilt capacity to be successful in life. Every manufacturer builds into his product the capacity to fulfil a function. For example, an iPad has an inbuilt capacity to satisfy the needs of mobile users who desire quick access to the internet, personal files and digital media on the go. The iPad's software is designed to let you create, access and manage extensive videos, images, music and other files. So, being able to fulfil this function, the iPad is seen as a success. However, for it to fulfil its function there are instructions or laws that one must follow to guarantee success – e.g., if the iPad is not charged (as instructed), it will not be able to perform its function. In the same way, we have been designed to succeed in life, but for us to succeed, we have to observe the laws of success. As you apply these laws to your life, you become the achiever you were born to be.

There are many laws of success. Of these, I have highlighted three, which we will be discussing in this chapter. I call these laws, 'The 3D Model' of achievement. The three 'D' model can guarantee you become the achiever you were born to be. This model will get you started and sustain you as you progress on the Path of Achievers.

DESIRE

"When you really want something to happen, the whole universe will conspire so that your wish comes true." — Paulo Coelho

Every journey begins with a first step. Before you can begin your journey on the Path of Achievers, you have to desire it first. All achievements and successes in life start with a desire. Desire is a strong wish for something, a want or aspiration. Whatever you desire wholeheartedly, with a definite purpose, you can have. If you desire something, you have an appetite for it. Intense desire or passion is what drives people into the significant accomplishments of this world. There is always 'something' within us, urging us on to bigger things. This 'something' can empower us to do anything we want to do, be anything we want to be, have anything we want to have — and we have this inner witness that this is possible. On the Path of Achievers, you must desire to be an achiever from the inside out. That is by looking inwardly and bringing out the best in you.

It is not enough to just have a desire; your desire should be specific and not general. Ask yourself this question: What is one thing that I desire above everything else in life? Life gives way to the person who really knows what he or she wants and goes for it.

DECISION

Decision is the next step to take on The 3D Model.
Decision can be defined in several ways:

Merriam-Webster — *a determination arrived at after consideration*
Longman — *a choice or judgment that you make after a period
of discussion or thought*
Definitions.net — *the act of making up your mind about something*

In simple terms, a decision is an act of making up your mind
about what you desire or want to do. Decision originally
comes from the Latin word decidere ("to determine"). This
step requires taking action. To act on a decision is to proceed
with determination. It is great to have a desire for something
or to be an achiever. But you have to go a step further by
making up your mind to get to your destination and take the
steps needed to get there.

You make thousands of decisions every day: what to wear,
what to drink, what to eat, how to spend your time, what
movie to watch, etc. However, making up your mind about
your life course is very important, as this will set you on a
path to your destiny. Your actions shape your life. If we want
to direct our lives, we must control our consistent actions. It
is not what we do once that shapes our future, but it is what
we do consistently. The secret of our future is in our daily
routine. If you want to know how you will turn out in life, pay
close attention to what you do consistently. And of course,
your actions are a result of your decisions.

For example, if you have exams coming up and decide to watch television or play video games for the majority of the time, and make little or no attempt to study, what do you think is going to happen? You might not pass the exams. If someone was watching you, I bet that they could predict what your results will be.

Decision determines what actions we take, who we become, and what our ultimate destination is in life. Everything that happens in your life, the events you are happy with and the events you are not happy with, began with a decision. This evidentially reveals how important decisions are. The decisions you are making right now will shape how you feel as well as who you are going to become in the years ahead.

All through history, decisions have shaped the destinies of the world, nations, people and individuals. Our world is full of people who made significant decisions that determined the course of history. An example is Abraham Lincoln's decision to issue the famous Proclamation of Emancipation, which gave freedom to people from African descent in the United States of America. Another example is Sir Winston Churchill's decision not to give up after Great Britain suffered a crippling attack by the German Luftwaffe during World War II. Churchill addressed the nation with these famous words: *"We shall defend our island, whatever the cost may be. We shall fight on the beaches, we shall fight on the landing grounds, we shall fight in the fields and in the streets, and we shall fight in the hills. We shall never surrender."*

Churchill's decision not to give up inspired the people of Great Britain to rise and defeat the larger, stronger German army. Individuals like Bill Gates, Steve Jobs, and many others, have changed the world. By deciding to stay with his passion and dreams, Bill Gates introduced software for computers and in doing so, pioneered technological innovation in the 20th Century.

In the words of Benjamin Disraeli, *"Man is not a creature of circumstances; circumstances are the creatures of men."* Your circumstances are a product of your decisions. You need to decide to subdue any unsuitable circumstances for your good. Decision is the pathway to power. It is the way of taking control of your life and turning everything around you for your good.

Three Decisions That Determine Your Destiny
1. *Your decision on what you focus on.*
2. *Your decision on how you define a given situation.*
3. *Your decision on what to do in a given situation.*

DESTINY
The Alchemist, a classic book by Paulo Coelho, follows the journey of a shepherd boy named Santiago. Believing a recurring dream to be prophetic, Santiago asks a fortune-teller in a nearby town what the dream meant. The woman interprets the dream as a prophecy, telling the boy that he will discover a treasure at the Egyptian Pyramids.

Early into his journey, he meets an old king named Melchizedek, or the king of Salem, who tells him to sell his sheep, so that he can travel to Egypt. This introduces the idea of a Personal Legend. Your Personal Legend "is what you have always wanted to accomplish. Everyone, when they are young, knows what their Personal Legend is."

Early in his arrival to Africa, a man who claims to be able to take Santiago to the Pyramids robs him of what money he has made from selling his sheep. Santiago then embarks on a long path of working for a crystal merchant so he can make enough money to fulfil his personal legend and go to the Pyramids.

Along the way, the boy meets an Englishman who has come in search of an alchemist and continues his travels in his new companion's company. When they reach an oasis, Santiago meets and falls in love with an Arabian girl named Fatima and proposes marriage. She promises to accept, but only after he completes his journey.

The boy then encounters a wise alchemist who also teaches him to realise his true self. Together, they risk a journey through the territory of warring tribes, where the boy is forced to demonstrate his oneness with "the soul of the world" by turning himself into a *simoom* (a hot desert wind) before he can proceed. When he begins digging within sight of the Pyramids, he is robbed yet again, but accidentally learns from the leader of the thieves that the treasure he sought all along was in the ruined church where he had his original dream.

This story, *The Alchemist* by Paulo Coelho, echoes the third step of the 3D MODEL of achievement – Destiny. Destiny has been viewed differently from several sources, including:

- *as a predetermined course of events. It is a predetermined future, whether in general or of an individual.*
- Cambridge Dictionary defines destiny as *the things that will happen in the future.*

Destiny suggests a destination. It highlights an end goal. There is a course of life for each one of us. Each one of us was born to take a unique and individual path; however, the decision is left entirely up to us whether we want to take that path or not. Just like there are no two persons on Earth with the same DNA and fingerprints, we all have unique paths for our lives. Your future is certain, but whether you arrive there is up to you.

As stated earlier, an achiever is someone who has discovered themself and is advancing towards a worthwhile goal. Real happiness comes from living from the inside out. Steadily working to accomplish your goals and advancing confidently in the direction of your life's purpose can achieve this. Throughout the history of mankind, different people who have found their place in time have led us from one thing to the other to give us the modern world we live in today.

To get to destiny, we must start with self-examination, which leads to self-discovery. When we discover ourselves, we learn what is inside of us. Throughout time, some people discovered their purpose and decided to make a difference and made the world a better place.

I must state that some people also found themselves on the wrong side of history and committed atrocities that were fatal to humanity. We determine destiny by our actions, and it is our repeated actions that set us on course towards or away from our destiny. The choice is yours. It is your decision that shapes your destiny. The beautiful thing is, it does not matter where you are on this journey because you can always change your course in life.

For example, there is an interesting account of Alfred Nobel, a pacifist at heart and an inventor by nature. A Swedish chemist, Nobel invented dynamite. However, the invention that he thought would end all wars became an extremely deadly product. In 1888, when Alfred's brother Ludvig died, a French newspaper mistakenly ran an obituary for Alfred, which called him the merchant of death. Not wanting to go down in history with such a horrible epitaph, Nobel created a will that soon shocked his relatives and established the now famous Nobel Prize.

This is an example of someone who put himself on the right side of history after realising that people saw him negatively. The Nobel Peace Prize is a prestigious award that celebrates the works of achievers around the world. In the words of Harry S. Truman, *"Actions are the seed of fate; deeds grow into destiny."* So, the action you decide will determine your destiny and your decisions father your actions.

In the world today, many problems need to be solved. We are still searching for the cure for HIV/AIDs, cancer and many other incurable diseases. You could be the one to bring the cure for HIV or cancer into the world. You are one of a kind with a unique calling. Make up your mind today that you will find your place in time and contribute significantly to the welfare of humanity.

In fulfilling our destiny, our decisions take us there. It is our decisions that are the subject of the state of our inner world. Our inner world is simply the condition or state of our mind.

Later on, we will discuss the role of the mind in fulfilling our destiny. We will discover that our outer world is a reflection of our inner world. Our achievements on the outside begin from the inside. Before we can truly create the life we want and deserve, we first have to create it from within us. Our inner world is equally as important as our outer world. By 'inner world' in the context of our discussion, I mean your mind. The consistent care of one's mind is essential to finding one's highest self and advancing in the direction of one's destiny. Advancing in the direction of destiny is living a purpose-driven life. Purpose is discovering your sense of destiny. In essence, understanding and observing the 3D Model will start you on the path of achievers to your destination.

REFLECTION

CHAPTER THREE

Know Your Purpose

A young man went to see the wise man in his village. "I don't know what to do with my life," he said. "How do I find my purpose?"

"Follow me," said the wise man.

Silently, they trudged along together to a faraway river where they found dozens of people mining for gold.

"There are three types of people here," the wise man said.

"What do you mean?" the young man inquired.

"There are those who strike gold straight away. Excited, they take their plunder, cash it in and live comfortably for the rest of their lives. Then there are those who mine for years. They know that there is gold here and they have seen others strike it and get rich, so they persist until they too find the gold that they've been searching for."

"What about the third group?" asked the young man.

"They are the individuals who get frustrated that they haven't found what they are looking for, so after a day, a week, a year or more, they give up, walk away and never find the gold."

Slightly confused, the young man asked, "What has this got

to do with finding my purpose?"

"Ah yes, the age-old question." The wise man smiled and looked his companion in the eyes. "There are those in life who look for their purpose and seem to find it almost immediately. From a young age, they have a clear sense of purpose and pursue their dreams with energy and enthusiasm. Some others must look a bit harder, perhaps for many years, but if they persist and keep looking, they will find something to live for. Finally, there are those who want to know their purpose, but they have become frustrated with the search and give up too soon, returning to a life of meaningless wandering."

"Can everyone find their purpose?"
"Is there gold in the river?"
"So, how do I find my own purpose?"
"Keep looking," said the wise man.

No matter where you are in search of your purpose, if you keep looking with genuine intent, you will find it. Each one of us was born with a purpose. There is a reason for your birth. There is a reason why you came to Earth. By extension, there is a reason why you were born to the parents you have. It is your duty to find out why you were born. We all have our unique callings in life and need to find out why we are here on Earth. For example, it could be that you were created to secure the next generation; to deliver innovative technology to produce clean water or clean energy. Everything has been created for a purpose. There is nothing in creation that is useless or exists for no reason. In the same vein, you have a purpose, and there is a reason why you were born. You came to this world with a purpose. To live a fulfilled life, you must find that purpose and live it out.

PURPOSE TOOLBOX

As we journey in life, we must be clear of some fundamental truths and principles. One such truth is purpose. Purpose simply means the 'why' of something. It is the reason for the existence of a thing. Everything in creation exists for a purpose. There is nothing in creation that is useless. If you consider the plants, they give us oxygen, which helps us to live. There are other examples of the usefulness of the things in nature and creation. Now you also exist for a reason and a purpose.

A common-sense approach to discover your purpose is observing your 'design.' Your design is your framework or make-up or how you are wired. You can observe the purpose of something by observing its design or frame. Think of a fan. If you look at the design of a fan, you could tell the manufacturer intended for it to circulate air.

Observing your 'Design'

There are a few models that could point you in the direction of your purpose. Have you taken the time to observe your design? Do you know what your talent is? What do you enjoy doing, or what are you good at? If not, the following models that I call 'tools' can help point you in the direction of your purpose. That is to say that you will have a glimpse of what you are supposed to do in life.

These tools are developed to help you discover your 'design', which invariably will help discover your purpose.

Tool 1 – The 'SHAPE MODEL'

The first model to consider is Rick Warren's SHAPE model. This is an indicator of the discovery of purpose. It is important to realise your SHAPE. SHAPE is an acronym for **Spiritual gifts, Heart, Abilities, Personality and Experiences**.

Spiritual Gifts

The Creator has given us all gifts. The manufacturer of a product puts into it special features to enable it to function effectively. In the same vein, we have unique abilities given to us by our manufacturer to enable us to serve our world effectively. Discovering these special abilities will point you in the direction of your purpose on Earth. It is essential to discover which gifts you have been endowed with. It helps you identify the most impactful and effective way to serve others.

Heart

The heart signifies your hopes, interests, ambitions, dreams and affections. Your heart represents the source of all your motivation – what you love to do and what you care about most. Your heart simply reveals your passion. This is with regard to what drives you or gives you the energy to wake up in the morning. What activities or interests provide you with a reason to serve, love, and fight for what is good? When you do what you are passionate about, you are most likely to be effective. Ultimately, when you do what you are wired for, you almost do it effortlessly. A lot of people hate their jobs but do it because of the money. I think it is priceless to do something that expresses your heart. Observing your passion is an indicator of what you were born to do.

Abilities

Your abilities are the natural talents you were born with. Each one of us is naturally good at something. Your path of achievements begins when you discover these skills and you start using them. To discover the purpose of your life, you should carefully examine what you are good at – and what you are not good at. There is a connection between what you were born to do and your capabilities. Whatever you were born to do, you were equipped to do it. Identifying your abilities will set you on a path towards your purpose. You do not have to waste your abilities. Identify them and use them. They were given to you for a reason. When you do not exercise your muscles, they weaken. In the same way, if you do not utilise the abilities and talents you have been given, they will remain untapped and unused and eventually will weaken. So, as you work on uncovering what you were born to do, another indicator is to look at your abilities, the things you are good at.

Personality

Your personality is a combination of characteristics that distinguish you as an individual. Scientists have suggested that some are introverts while others are extroverts. Some people like routine and others like variety. Some are analytical, while others have spatial intelligence. Some people work best when given an individual assignment, while others work better in a team. All types of personalities are relevant. There are no right or wrong temperaments when it comes to your purpose. The world would be a very boring place if we were all the same. Each one of us has a personality that reveals seed-talent. We should cultivate our natural characteristics and start embracing them so that we can make a difference to the world around us.

Experiences

Experience is the process of growing in knowledge from doing, seeing, or feeling things. Experience is one of life's greatest teachers. It is often our experiences that shape us into the men and women we ought to be. And sometimes it can be experience that indicates purpose and prepares you to do those things that you were born to do. You have been shaped by your experiences in life, whether good or bad. There are various questions and meditations that arise when we examine the various components that make up our individual experiences.

Family experiences: What did you learn growing up in your family?

Educational experiences: What were your favourite subjects in school?

Vocational experiences: What jobs have you been most effective in and enjoyed most? Painful experiences:

What problems, hurts, thorns and trials have you learned from? All these experiences have moulded you to become the person you are today, and sometimes these

experiences suggest what you were born to do and the solutions you were born to solve.

Tool 2 – The 'SIGN MODEL'

SIGN is an acronym initially coined by Marcus Buckingham. It stands for **Success, Instincts, Growth and Needs.** SIGN is designed to help you organise and remember the key indicators of your true strength. Discovering your true strength indicates your design.

Success

Buckingham introduces the first letter in his SIGN model with a proposition: "If I were to ask you to describe your strengths, you would more than likely begin with those things at which you feel successful in and frankly, this is a sensible place to start. For something to be labelled a strength, you must have some ability in it and a proven track record. Your success is the best indicator of your ability. It is about how effective you are at an activity. Recognising an area you feel most successful in is a reliable indicator of a strength."

Instinct

Another indication of strength is when you feel drawn to a specific activity. Buckingham explains that your strengths have an "I can't help but" quality to them. "You can not quite articulate why, but you find yourself drawn to certain activities repeatedly. Even though you may be hesitant to do them, with thoughts of inferiority or doubt, you feel a pull towards them."

Growth

Strengths are where you grow the most. According to Buckingham, "by now, you know that the biological underpinnings of your strengths are the presence of thick branches of synaptic connections. When you engage in an activity that you are wired for, you grow quickly. You also know that because of nature's habit of piggybacking on existing infrastructure, you will grow the newest synaptic connections in those areas where you already have the most existing ones. Here you will learn the most, come up with the newest ideas, and have the best insights."

Needs

The Needs SIGN is an indicator of the strengths that are essential to society's progress. It is unique to the individual as their innate ability or strength is what resolves the issues within our wider society and global community. Filling that void within you meets a need in society, and thus gives you a sense of fulfilment. Buckingham observes that "[w]hile the Instinct sign refers to how you feel before you do the activity, and the Growth sign is to your feelings during the activity, the Needs sign points to how you feel right after you have done it."

EXERCISE

Use the following key questions to help understand your true strength:

- **What are your strengths?**

- **Do you spend more time growing your strengths or fixing your weaknesses?**

- **How can you find ways to spend more time exercising your strengths each day?**

Tool 3 – The 'DESIGN Model'

The 'DESIGN Model' is a model I developed to help the people to see a glimpse of their purpose for being. 'DESIGN' is an acronym for **Desire, Enthusiasm, Strength, Irritation, Gratification, and Need.** These various indicators can point you in the direction of your purpose.

Desire

Desire is a strong indicator of purpose. Desire can be described as a 'longing', 'yearning', 'wishing' or 'wanting' for something. It brings to light the seeds in us. Desire in its purest form is the **'expressions of seeds'.** Each one of us has been wired with a unique genetic predisposition to be and to do something fluently. We came to Earth with unique gifts and talents, and that has been echoed out of our heart through our desires. For example, an apple tree is trapped in an apple seed. At the seed level, the tree longs and desires to be the tree it is supposed to be. However, it must go through the process of *becoming.* In the same vein, we all have seeds in us, the seed of a medical doctor, engineer, lawyer, entrepreneur, teacher, and so forth. These seeds usually express themselves in our desires. Paying attention to your desires is paying attention to the seeds in you. Sometimes there are desires that never go away unless you fulfil them. This is a good sign of purpose.

```
EXERCISE
```

- **Write down all the desires of your heart until you feel you've emptied yourself.**

- **Seek out the desires that resonate with you.**

- **Start filtering and organising your desires in order of priorities, and design a plan to fulfil them.**

Enthusiasm

Enthusiasm is an indicator of your purpose. According to Merriam-Webster's Dictionary, enthusiasm is *"something inspiring zeal or fervour,"* something that breathes passion. When you are enthusiastic about something, you come alive, and the activity that you are involved in makes your juices flow. You get absorbed in it and the time just goes. Sometimes you forget to eat until you are reminded to do so. You are eager to do these things. Enthusiasm suggests an intense interest in something which can be seen as passion. It is a driving or overpowering feeling. It is a strong liking for or devotion to an activity. You can identify your life's purpose by observing what really moves you or what you feel wholly devoted to. You can be enthusiastic about computers and software, like Bill Gates. As a result, he created Microsoft for the world. Enthusiasm captures your attention. It is energetic, eager, and when these signs are showing as a result of a given activity, it is one of the best indicators of purpose.

Strength

I read a story of three pelicans who were flying to a popular lake. As they travelled, they were each lost in thought.

The first pelican thought, *I love my beak. It's magnificent. No other bird has a beak quite like mine. When I get to the lake, I'm going to parade along the bank, showing off my beautiful beak — and all of the other birds will be jealous!*

The second pelican thought, *I love my beak, and I need to protect it. I can't afford for it to get damaged, so I'm going only to catch small fish in shallow waters. I know I can do more, but it's too risky.*

The third pelican thought, *I love my beak. It's a beauty, and I'm going to push the limits and get the most out of it. I'm going to become the best catcher of fish in the lake. I've been given this beak for a reason, so I'm going to work hard and catch the biggest fish out there!*

We have all been given unique talents, experiences and attributes for a reason. We need to develop them fully and use them to their maximum capacity. We are each here to make a positive difference to the world around us and are all equipped for the task.

You are gifted. No one on Earth is talentless. There is a seed-talent in every soul on Earth. The issue is always the discovery and developments of those unique talents. You have special abilities, which is a gift you can maximise to serve the world and thereby make a difference in the world.

When you identify the proficiency, skill or talent in you, it is an indicator of purpose based on your design. As you identify this gift, serve the world with it, and it will cause your light to shine.

Irritation

In your search for your life's purpose, another indicator you can observe is, whatever irritates you. According to Merriam-Webster's Dictionary, to irritate is *"to provoke impatience, anger or displeasure in."* This feeling of displeasure can be used to an advantage. Let's say you were born to be an event organiser, but you are yet to realise it. When you attend an event, you tend to get annoyed or irritated when things appear not to be well-organised, though others might not see the flaws. You might struggle to enjoy the event and might end up correcting a thing or two. If these things happen to you, you might have discovered something very special about yourself. You have the seed-talent of an event organiser, and that could point you towards your life's aim.

Gratification

Gratification is a source of satisfaction or great pleasure. It is doing something that you find rewarding without monetary motivation. It is doing something you love so much that you do not mind doing it for free. This is because your motivation for doing this stems from within you and not externally. This is a good sign of gratification. Let's take someone who loves to bake. Their passion for baking is so overwhelming that whether or not they are being paid to bake for an occasion, they would still spend that time and effort into creating a masterpiece that is worth much. The satisfaction they get from being able to express themselves in a beautiful creation goes beyond making a business transaction. A popular adage affirms: *"Find something you like doing so much that you'd gladly do it for nothing, and if you learn to do it well, someday people will be happy to pay you for it."* Gratification suggests you just enjoy doing it and is an indicator of joy. There is a distinct difference between joy and happiness. Joy stems from deep within you, whereas happiness is generally based on circumstances. Theopedia defines joy as *"a state of mind and an orientation of the heart. It is a settled state of contentment, confidence and hope."* This shows that joy describes an experience from the inside out. It suggests how you can become absorbed in an activity that

57

you find yourself loving. Whatever you do that excites you, whatever brings you joy and satisfaction, is an indicator of purpose.

Need

You were born to meet a need in society. According to Merriam-Webster's Dictionary, a need is *"a necessary duty, an obligation."* It suggests you have a duty to the world, which is an obligation; there is something you ought to do, and only you can do it. There is something in you that the world needs. You came to Earth with a solution to meet a need that you can solve. Identifying that need and meeting it is basically doing what you were born to do and giving the world what you were created to give it. You are designed to solve the problem you were born to solve. By observing your design, you will identify your gift, which is an inherent capacity to fulfil a function that meets a need in creation. When it comes to meeting needs in society, it is the gift you release that solves the problem. In other words, there is something in you that the world needs and that thing is meant to solve a specific problem. This goes a long way to suggest that you are valuable. This world needs what you have, but you have to identify what you have to serve the world with it, and by doing so, you will be meeting a need in society. You have the seed of solutions to a need in you. Unleash it to meet that need. Meeting the need in society affirms that you are doing what you were born to do. You are living out your purpose.

LIVING OUT YOUR PURPOSE (UNFOLDING YOUR PATH)

Purpose reveals your innate reason for living. When you discover it; you will start living from the inside out, and this gives you internal locus of control. As an individual, when you discover your purpose, you must go to the next stage of living it out to manifest your true achievement in life and become fulfilled.

After you have discovered a definite purpose for your journey in life, the next important thing is to plan on how you are going to get to your destination and fulfil your purpose. Charting your course in life includes developing the following:

Personal Vision Statement

As you begin to uncover your purpose, it gives you an idea of what you should be doing and how you are going to do it. Even if you are still discovering your purpose, you should begin crafting a vision statement.

A vision is a picture of a desired future. You can see how things could be in the future. It holds you accountable for the choices you make about your life. A good vision statement will include all areas of your life, including family, academic, health and fitness, personal development, business, recreational, finances, and so on. Your personal vision statement is something you write by yourself from your heart so that it resonates with you and helps you live a certain way as you work towards your vision in life. Your personal vision does not remove distraction. It inspires you to focus on what matters. Vision provides clarity for the future - directing you to a place while your attention is in the present. Your personal vision can be a sentence or a paragraph. Allow your vision to paint a mental picture of your life from 3, 5 or even 20 years from now.

Examples of Personal Vision Statement

Sir Richard Branson's vision statement can be summarised as: *"To have fun in [my] journey through life and learn from [my] mistakes."*

Oprah Winfrey's vision is: *"To be a teacher. And to be known for inspiring my students to be more than they thought they could be."*
(Please see the Resource Page for a template of a Personal Vision Statement Plan).

Personal Mission Statement

It is crucial that you design a Mission Statement which outlines your general assignment in life. A Mission Statement is an inspiring and empowering document that affirms your commitment to a specific personal sense of purpose. This encapsulates the meaning for your life, your values, desirable character traits, roles you will play in your life and your goals, which ultimately paints a picture of your legacy.
(Please see Resource Page for the Personal Mission Statement Template).

Personal Development Plan

A Personal Development Plan is a clearly-defined path you will take to reach your vision. It charts your course of life, giving you an idea of things you need to do and possible resources that you will need on your journey.

One cannot build a life without a definite plan of what you are going to do and how you are going to do it. It can be likened to an architect building a house and suggesting they do not need a plan, instead choosing to figure things out as they go along. This is not possible.

We often have desires, dreams and goals for our future, but rarely do we take the time to consider them. A plan helps you to work out the details, foresee any potential challenges and offers clarity on how things could turn out.
(Please see the Resource Page for a template of a Personal Development Plan).

Goal setting, Goal getting

Goals are targets we set to achieve at certain stages of our lives. Setting a goal requires planning and commitment. After you have established your goals, you have to be willing to put the work in to achieve your desired end. Pablo Picasso said, *"Our goals can only be reached through a vehicle of a plan in which we must fervently believe, and upon which we must vigorously act. There is no other route to success."*

Goal setting and goal getting promote long-term vision. It focuses on intention, desire, acquisition of knowledge, and supports the organisation of resources. You can set a range of goals varying from short-term to long-term goals. Achieving your goals is simply reaching one target after the other, towards your definite purpose in life.

Here are five simple steps for achieving your goals:
Step 1: Write your goal down. The discipline of writing down your goal is a step towards making it happen. When you document your thoughts, it helps you to get down to specifics.

Step 2: Form a clear mental image of the outcome you desire. The clearer the mental picture, the more effective the process will be. Picturing your goal will help you to achieve it.

Step 3: Give a timeline to your goal. Timelines help you to prioritise as well as help you to focus your energy in reaching your goal.

Step 4: Get a motivating factor. Tell people about your goal. For example, if your goal is to get a good grade in school, this can help to keep you accountable as other people can help track your progress. Telling people will put some positive pressure on you to achieve your goal by the given deadline.
Step 5: Be consistent. Keeping your goal in focus is key to realising it. Review your goals daily. A technique that can support the daily review of your goals is to write it on your vision board or in your journal.

Step 5: Be consistent. Keeping your goal in focus is key to realising it. Review your goals daily. Use a vision board or a journal to measure your progress.

REFLECTION

CHAPTER FOUR

Discover Yourself

A chicken farmer found an eagle's egg. He put it with his chickens and soon the egg hatched. The young eagle grew up with all the other chickens, and whatever they did, the eagle did too. The eagle thought it was a chicken, just like them. Since the chickens could only fly for a short distance, the eagle also learnt to fly for a short distance. The eagle thought that was what it was supposed to do, and could do. Eventually, that was all the eagle was able to do. One day the eagle saw a bird flying high above him. The eagle was very impressed.

"Who is that?" the eagle asked the hens around.

"That's the eagle, the king of the birds," said the hens. "They belong to the sky. We belong on the ground because we are just chickens."

The eagle grew up doing what chickens do, living like a chicken, and believing it was a chicken.

Mr Fulton, a zoologist, visited the chicken farm and was surprised to see the eagle strutting around the chicken coop, pecking at the ground, and acting very much like a chicken. The farmer explained to Mr Fulton that this bird was no longer an eagle. It was now a chicken because it had been trained to be a chicken and believed that it was a chicken. Mr Fulton knew that this was an erroneous mistake as there was so much more to this magnificent bird. Despite the eagle's environment and upbringing, it was born an eagle and had the heart of an eagle, and nothing could change that.

Mr Fulton lifted the eagle onto the fence surrounding the chicken coop and said, "You are an eagle! Stretch out your wings and fly!"

The eagle moved slightly, looked at Mr Fulton, then glanced down at its home among the other chickens and jumped off the fence and continued doing what chickens do.

The farmer was satisfied. "I told you it's a chicken!"

Mr Fulton returned the next day and tried again to convince the farmer that the eagle was born for something greater. He took the eagle to the top of the farmhouse and spoke to it: "You are an eagle! Stretch out your wings and fly!" The large bird looked at him, then again down into the chicken coop. The eagle jumped from his arm onto the roof of the farmhouse.

Knowing what an eagle is capable of, Mr Fulton asked the farmer to let him try one more time. He would return the next day and prove that this bird was indeed an eagle.

The farmer was convinced otherwise. "It's a chicken!" he said. Mr Fulton returned the next morning to the chicken farm and took the eagle and the farmer up to a high mountain far away from the chicken coop. With the eagle on his arm, he pointed it above his head towards the sun's beckoning light. "You are an eagle!" he said. "You belong to the sky and not on the ground! Stretch your wings and fly!"

This time the eagle stared skyward into the bright sun, straightened its large body, and stretched its massive wings. The eagle's wings moved slowly at first, then surely and powerfully, with the mighty screech of an eagle, it flew.

Just like the eagle, you need to discover your intrinsic self, looking beyond your environment, conditions and the words of others.

Lao Tzu rightly said: *"Knowing others is intelligence; knowing yourself is true wisdom. Mastering others is strength; mastering yourself is true power."*

It is interesting how we are keen on knowing people from different walks of life, yet the one person we must know, we ignore. Today, Social Media is a platform that is thriving. I believe it is because we are social beings, and we like to connect and know people. On the contrary, we do less to know ourselves. We fail to understand that you cannot really know people and have a good relationship with them if we do not have a good self-concept. As Aristotle rightly puts it, *"All friendly feelings for others are an extension of a man's feelings for himself."*

The average person in the world does not know who they are. Knowing yourself is an important aspect of your being. It comes with a lot of great benefits – emotional, psychological and physical. It makes you live congruently with your true self, which is good for your health and success. Life becomes sweet when you know who you are and what you are made of. If you are going to live with someone all your life, then it is worth knowing who that person is. You are going to live with yourself for the rest of your life, so take an interest in knowing and understanding 'you'.

There is a quiet frustration that lives in your heart when you do not know yourself. You may choose to live with it and ignore it – or you may choose to start getting to know yourself and reap the full benefits. Just as it is impossible to reach your destination when you do not know where you are in life, it is also challenging to become the achiever you were born to be when you do not know who you are in life.

This is a discussion of self-knowledge, which is important because there are so many things you could learn about yourself. But in the context of our discussion, when we talk about knowing yourself, we are dealing with understanding your inner self, i.e. emotionally or psychologically. You can choose to learn and focus on external attributes of yourself but decide to go deeper and learn about your innate qualities.

Understanding Yourself

As we seek to understand ourselves, let's start by understanding our inner world. When we understand ourselves, we will know who we are and what we can do to help us live from the inside out. Most of the challenges we face are due to inauthentic living where people are living incongruently to their true nature or self. To start living authentically, you must understand yourself. For example, if you are a fish and you enter a competition to climb a tree, there is no way you can win. Understanding yourself starts by knowing yourself, and this includes, but is not limited to, understanding your capabilities, expertise, personal values; your interests, temperament, goals; your life mission, strengths, weaknesses and skills.

We live in two worlds: the inner world and the outer world. Our ability to engage in those two worlds is what results in our achievements in life. Our inner world is made up of our **mind, will and emotions**. This is where we train ourselves to live successfully in life. Our outer world is the physical world we make contact with on the outside. It reflects our inner world. Therefore, when we enrich our inner world, it enhances our outer world. It will make us more effective and efficient in whatever we do. This experience of life is based on the principle of living from the inside out.

Life is governed by principles. We must understand that there are laws in nature that govern the order of things. For example, we have the law of gravity that states that what goes up must come down. We also have life principles that govern how life works and the results that are achieved.

What is 'Your Inner World'?

Our inner world is likened to the inner mechanism of things. For example, the inner world is like the motherboard of your laptop. Our inner world affects our outer reality. With our inner operative mechanisms, we can enhance our external performance or behaviours. Our inner world is our inner self – that is our true self (your mind, will and emotions).

People do not pay attention to their inner world because they are so focussed on the outer world. What people describe as the 'real world' is the outer world, but on the contrary, the real world is the inner world. This is because the inner world causes them to see the outer world in a particular way. The inner world is the control centre of our lives. Although it is not tangible, your inner world does exist. When we learn to understand this internal mechanism, it will give us a better outlook on life.

The subject of our inner world was reflected in the writings of great philosophers like Augustine, Plato, and Aristotle. They each knew something about inner self where meaning is born, and inner thoughts guide our outward actions. Your inner world is the place where you gain insight to uncover your true self and purpose in life to operate in the world. Our outer world is a reflection of our inner world, so I encourage you to spend time building your inner world so that your outer world will flourish. This can be likened to a garden that you tend to, beautifully cultivating the bulbs each day to become a glorious flower.

Exercises for Getting to Know Yourself Better

When you begin your journey of self-knowledge, there are so many things you can learn, including your temperaments, capabilities, expertise, personal values, interests, your life's mission, and so on.

The process of self-discovery involves taking several personal ventures. There are both conventional and unconventional ways of knowing yourself. A conventional way is taking a personality test to ascertain certain features you have. Amongst the myriad of unconventional approaches to knowing yourself are self-reflection, quiet time (introspection), seeking meaning, serving others and journaling.

Taking a Personality Test

These are structured, online assessments that can support your quest to understand your personality. Understanding your personality type can provide the key to recognising why you have tendencies to act or react in a certain way. It can also help you to understand your environment and how to be effective in that environment. There are several tools widely used, including *the Myers Briggs Type Indicator (MBTI), The Enneagram and Clifton Strength.*
(Please see the Resource Page for links to these tools).

Self-Reflection

"The journey into self-love and self-acceptance must begin with self-examination. Until you take the journey of self-reflection, it is almost impossible to grow or learn in life." – Iyanla Vanzant

Self-reflection is the process of engaging in an introspective exercise. It is about understanding yourself, your thought process, your values and your capabilities. It is like looking into a mirror and describing what you see. It is a form of personal analysis to help you live in alignment with your true self. Ultimately, to live authentically. Self-reflection is a valuable exercise to get to know yourself.

How to Self-Reflect

The idea is to have time in solitude and engage in introspection.
i. Finding a solitary place is required for this exercise. You can take a walk in the park, sit in a comfortable place in a grassy area, lie on your bed, or find a quiet place in your house where you can be alone.
ii. Relax and be calm. You can aid this step by controlling your breathing. You want to be in a calm and peaceful state and not in an unsettled state.
iii. When you have achieved this level of calmness, then ask yourself questions to discover yourself.

- Who am I?
- Why was I born?
- What can I do?
- What are 5-10 traits that I believe define who I am?
- If I could live my life once more, what would I do differently?
- What makes me feel joyful?
- What do I like about myself and what would I like to change?

Remember that the questions above are examples. You are not limited to them.

Seek Meaning

"Life is never made unbearable by circumstances, but only by lack of meaning and purpose." — Viktor E. Frankl

As we seek to find meaning in our lives, we invariably get to know ourselves. Essentially, to find ourselves, we must all seek out our sense of purpose in life. Each one of us came to this world to fulfil a purpose (as mentioned in Chapter 3), and as we seek to know and fulfil our purpose on Earth, we get to know ourselves.

Journaling

Journaling is the practice of keeping a diary to write down your thoughts, feelings, experiences and the events in your life. You can write in your journal as often as you want. Journaling is a great way to monitor your consciousness and the events of your life. This exercise can help you understand your trend of thoughts and ideas and help identify your narrative. It can help distinguish your inner voice from the voices around. It is a great way to learn about and understand yourself.

The 5 Self-Knowledge Structure

As you attain self-knowledge, it will help you to be conscious of yourself in a profound way. In the process of self-discovery, there are essential concepts we ought to know and understand.

Self-Awareness

Self-awareness is the capacity for introspection and the ability to recognise one's self as an individual separate from the environment and other individuals. Psychologist Daniel Goleman, proposed a popular definition of self-awareness in his best-selling book, Emotional Intelligence: "[It is] knowing one's internal states, preference, resources, and intuitions." This definition places more emphasis on the ability to monitor our inner world, our thoughts and emotions as they arise.

Self-Concept
The term self-concept is a general term used to refer to how people think about, evaluate or perceive themselves. It can be viewed as the belief you have about yourself.

Self-Worth
Self-worth is the belief that you are valuable. If you have no self-worth, then you do not believe that you are deserving of much in life. However, if you are confident about your self-worth, you would believe and act like you are deserving of respect, honour and love.

Self-Image
Self-image is how we see ourselves. This is the picture in your mind about yourself, whether you see yourself as someone who is always excelling in everything you do, or whether you see yourself as being average in society.

Self-Actualisation
Self-actualisation has also been described as the psychological process of maximising the use of a person's abilities and resources. This process may vary from one person to another. Self-actualisation is the discovery and realisation of one's potential.

REFLECTION

CHAPTER FIVE

Be Yourself

The privilege of a lifetime is to
become who you truly are.
– Carl Jung

Can an apple seed grow into a mango fruit? If your answer is no, you are right.

But did you know that humans sometimes become what they are not? Ralph Waldo Emerson observed that *"to be yourself in a world that is constantly trying to make you something else, is the greatest accomplishment."* Be yourself. Become who you already are on the inside. Remember, the seed of everything is 'in itself' – *the seed of itself is in itself.* For example, an apple seed becomes an apple tree and then becomes an apple fruit, and the cycle continues.

Being yourself is living your authentic life. No one wants to be played, fooled or deceived. Everyone wants to connect with people who are genuine and real. Many people are not themselves as they have taken on the ideas of other people and are living very inauthentic lives. However, learning to live authentically will bring you great results. Shakespeare said, *"to thine own self be true."* Be yourself, be true to yourself, do not engage in self-deception.

Being yourself is the quality of being real or true. It is the degree to which an individual's actions are congruent with their beliefs and desires. The conscious self is seen as coming to terms with being in the material world and with encountering external forces, pressures, and influences which are very different from itself but still staying true to itself.

The most beautiful thing you will ever witness in your life is when you begin to unfold into the person you were born to be. Albert Einstein once said: *"Everybody is a genius. But if you judge a fish by its ability to climb a tree, it will live its whole life believing that it is stupid."*

Oscar Wilde said, *"Be yourself; everyone else is already taken."* It is a basic summation of a truth. Yet you can not be yourself if you do not know, understand, and accept yourself first. This is true of everything, like seeds in nature. They have a specific potential coded into them for them to be themselves. They ought to produce after their kind — an acorn will grow into a mighty oak tree; a chicken's egg into a hen or rooster. Given the right conditions, environment, care and nourishment, that seed will grow into its potential.

We each come into this life with a specific potential coded within us, something we are born to fulfil. Like the acorn, we have everything we need within us to fulfil our specific potential. All we need to do is to become what we already are. But we can only reach that if our unique potential is recognised, nurtured and we receive the right conditions, environment and nourishment that will protect and grow us into who we are yet to become.

Society conditions you to live a 'normal' life, becoming what it wants you to be instead of what you are supposed to be. The world has a way in which it tries to imprint its definition of what life should be. Your parents, your friends, your work colleagues, the media, and your environment will try to impose upon you the mediocre way of life. You will be conditioned to be normal, to follow the beaten path, to live in self-betrayal, to live a lie, and to be like everyone else, just getting by, paying your bills and looking forward to pension schemes.

Become aware of your truth and go confidently in the right direction that you desire. Joseph Curiale echoed this truth by stating: *"If you're not living your truth, you're living a lie."* You can continue to live small by living in the shadow of others, or just being like everyone else, and doing what everyone else is doing daily (binge-watching shows and scrolling aimlessly on social media platforms). Or you can step up, examine your life and live a life of meaning.

Go inward and discover your truth. Inward is where the answers lie. If you look within yourself, you will find what you seek.

The Keys to Being Yourself

Discovering Your Truth

Probably the hardest part of being yourself is discovering what your truth is. To discover your truth, you have to listen to your inner self, and usually, this happens when you are alone. You know who you are as a person; you know what makes your heart fill with joy and what makes you smile. If you ignore society and individual's expectations, definitions, and judgements, you will become aware of this truth within you.

Live Your Truth!

Once you have recognised your truth and embraced your individuality, you will realise that living your truth will ultimately free you. You will realise that you are confident, powerful and also realise that you will become more authentic when communicating with others and yourself!

Living your truth will free you from seeking validation from other people because you will recognise your own self-worth. You will begin to feel less guilty for investing in yourself and prioritising your aspirations and goals. You owe it to yourself to make sure you are mentally and emotionally healthy.

Develop and express your individuality. Whether it is your sense of style or even your manner of speaking, if your preferred way of doing something strays from the mainstream and produces positive outcomes, then be proud of it. Be a character, not a type. Be your unique self, not one of the masses.

Probing Questions:

What do I stand for?

What are my core values?

What are my strengths and weaknesses?

What limiting beliefs do I have about myself?

Do I have personal standards and boundaries?

What makes me happy, and how can I have more of this?

What does my heart secretly long for?

If you're not living your truth...

Your life seems to be out of alignment.

You're not stable.

You're unclear about what to do with your life and don't know where to start changing it.

You don't understand why nothing seems to be going your way.

You feel abandoned – alone, adrift, disconnected, lost.

You can't see any possibilities, feel hopeless, directionless.

You're critical, frustrated, sad – and nothing seems enjoyable.

You're overly dependent on others for credibility.

Your self-worth is from external variables.

If you're living your truth...

You have an innate reason for living.

You are progressively becoming what you were born to be.

You have a vision for your life.

You'll be better prepared to handle adversity and have more resilience.

You won't need others' approval to validate your worth.

You'll have the confidence to speak and live your truth.

You'll no longer feel guilty taking care of yourself.

You'll trust life more so you can let go of pushing and striving to make things happen.

You'll experience a much greater sense of assurance that everything is going to be okay.

You'll have a realistic perception of reality.

You'll be accepting of yourself and other people.

You feel fulfilled as you go about your work.

You sense and know that you are on the Path of Achievers.

When you are living authentically, you express your emotions freely and clearly and have a realistic perception of reality. You accept yourself and other people. **Think Inward, Look Outward** – this means living 'from the inside out' and not 'from the outside in.' Make sure everything you do is a product of your own conclusion.

Be proud of who you are! You are given one life, and you can cherish it so much more when you live truthfully. We are always told to tell the truth, so I do not see the problem with being especially true to ourselves. Become yourself. Become who you were born to be.

REFLECTION

CHAPTER SIX

Enhance Yourself

S ome people have become victims of their inner world (mind, emotion and will) as opposed to using it as their tools to be effective in life. Let's take your will as an example. Your will should help you to live effectively. However, some have become victims of their will. They are not able to control their impulses, e.g., an addict acts on impulses as opposed to conscious decisions. Enhancing yourself means programming your inner world to live effectively.

The **'MEW'** model is used to enrich the achievements you have not yet unlocked. The model deals with the exploration of **Mind, Emotions and Will**. These faculties form the control centre of our inner world, and understanding this helps us to live authentically and become true achievers. All the faculties of our inner world are to serve us as they are tools for being effective in life. Overcoming problems you may encounter, such as addictive behaviours or anger issues, are connected to these three faculties of human nature – mind, emotions and will (MEW). This model is designed to solve the problems of humans, such as rage and violence, and so on.

MIND

The human mind has been deconstructed, explored and the subject of discourse by a plethora of experts from a range of backgrounds including scientists, doctors, philosophers, and psychologists. Yet, they do not have a common conclusion of where the mind is located, and some suggest the mind is the product of brain activity. The brain is the physical substance, and the mind is the conscious product of those firing neurons.

But growing evidence shows that the mind goes beyond the physical workings of your brain. The mind is the seat of consciousness, and if that is the case, it goes beyond brain activity. In medical science, evidence shows that the brain can be fully functional even when an individual is not conscious. This suggests that there is a distinct difference between the mind (the seat of consciousness) and the brain.

The mind is the faculty of a person's thoughts and reasoning. The mind holds the power of imagination, recognition and appreciation, and is responsible for processing feelings and emotions, resulting in attitudes and actions. We have a conscious and subconscious mind. The mind is typically described as consciousness, but it has been said that the conscious part represents only a fraction of the whole mind and that most of the mind's activity lies in the realm of the subconscious. The conscious mind controls the physical senses (sight, smell, touch, vision and taste). The subconscious part of the mind governs the involuntary actions. For example, you are not thinking about trying to breathe while reading this book. It is an automatic action or activity governed by the subconscious mind.

It has been stated that great inventions, creative writers, renowned scientists and outstanding wise people learned to draw from their subconscious mind. Sir Isaac Newton acquired his vast knowledge of mathematics and physics with no conscious effort but instead drew on inspirations from his subconscious mind. Our ability to make proper and full use of mind power will determine our level of achievement in life. You can harness the power of your mind through a concentrated effort. This can be achieved by focusing your full attention on the task at hand and attesting to the fact that whatever could be achieved in your life will come from within you.

How the Mind Works
The mind is a magnificent faculty in us. It is a tool to accelerate our mission in the world and to help us create the life we want or aspire to. Psychologists state that on average, we use only ten percent of our mental power. In essence, there are deposits of energy which can be described as treasures in the mind that if brought to the surface will gain us an incredible wealth of influence and control of our environment. Those deposits of energies and treasures represent our mental power. All through the ages, people using their mind have learnt to adapt and to outgrow their limitations. From the

Stone Age to the Iron Age to the Golden Age to the Mental Age and now the Digital Age, we have moved from one dispensation to another by the use of the mind.

By using their minds, people have come up with great inventions and technology — airplanes, trains, cars, computers, the Internet, and so on. Through the mind, we have made machines to do the work of millions of domestic animals and billions of hands. Today, the Internet offers us an untethered and instant connection to the rest of the world and reduces our manual workload. We have access to everything and anything we want online from buying groceries to finding potential spouses. Great inventions and innovations like the Internet have come about as the brainchild of people.

Changing Your Input

When we cultivate and nurture the fertile garden of our minds, it will blossom and give us results beyond our expectation. We will attain life mastery when we can gain control of our minds. By being able to control our thoughts, we can decide what we do better. This will ultimately give us control of our lives. When we dedicate ourselves to transforming our inner world by transforming our minds, our lives will quickly shift from the ordinary into the realm of the extraordinary.

We must learn to cultivate the fertile garden of our minds. We must always ensure that we are keeping our minds healthy and devoid of contamination and corruption. We have to stand at the gates of our minds and assess the information we let in. You are who you are because of what you allow to enter your mind; but until you control and change what enters your mind, you cannot change your outer reality.

This can be achieved by regulating the thoughts that enter your mind, e.g., the things you read, watch and listen to in your everyday life. You need to be conscious of the thoughts you entertain in your mind. It is crucial to concentrate on positive thoughts and disregard any negative thoughts. To tame your mind, it takes the two major gates or entering points; these are your eyes and your ears. Anyone or anything that controls what you watch and listen to controls your life because they are the gateways to your inner world.

In the words of Albert Einstein, "*My mind is my office*" because that is where the activity goes on. Your mind is the seat of your **thoughts, intellect and imagination**. These are great forces in your mind. In this space, you can master the art of 'mind control.' By enriching your inner world, you will enhance your outer world to create the life you want and deserve. Let's look further into the features of the mind. By that, I mean the 'conscious mind' – **THOUGHTS, INTELLECT AND IMAGINATION**.

THOUGHTS

Thoughts are words, ideas, or images that come into your mind. These images or ideas can be created, recalled, reviewed or processed for meaning, reason, language or expression. They could be the product of an individual's aims, wishes, or desires as a result of stimuli in the environment. Thoughts are a conscious, mental construction of your mind-based on imagination, information or stimuli. They can influence your emotion. They are powerful. Thoughts are like a guest. Even after a guest has left, the impact of their presence remains, and it can have an impact on you and others.

Thoughts are living things. They start as seeds in your mind and later take on a life of their own. They draw power from you to cause the picture in your mind to manifest. When thoughts are employed wrongly, they can obstruct your progress towards becoming the achiever you were born to be. Sometimes all it takes to have a great future is to change the way you think.

No one can experience a real change in their life until they change the way they think. Our outside world is a result of the state of our inner world. We can mould our surroundings ourselves by directing our thoughts towards the goal we have in mind. As Robert Collier rightly said, *"The world without is but a reflection of that world within."*

We must choose positive thoughts that reflect thoughts of peace, thoughts of abundance, of good health, of achievements. Like William James said, *"The greatest discovery of my generation is that human beings can alter their lives by altering their attitudes of mind."*

By employing our thoughts rightly, we can achieve outstanding results in life. Everything we see around us started as an idea in the mind. The houses, skyscrapers, cathedrals, the computers, the Internet — all started in the mind of someone as an idea. They conceived these great projects first in their minds, pictured them vividly, which enabled them to overcome obstacles to realise their dreams.

INTELLECT

Intellect is a product of the mind. It is a term used in studies of the human mind. Intellect refers to one's ability to come to correct conclusions about what is true or false and how to solve problems. Intellect is the ability to understand and to think logically.

Intellect is a brand of intelligence and can be described as the capacity for thinking and acquiring knowledge. It also suggests the activity of reasoning and comprehension of things objectively, especially abstract ideas. This is a very valuable faculty that helps us to make sense of the things around us and facilitates our desire to learn. Our ability to learn supports us to deal with our circumstances intelligently and produce results in everything that we do. Intellect is needed to achieve success in life.

Intellect governs our capacity to reason, plan, comprehend ideas, think abstractly and learn. It is made up of **wisdom, knowledge and instruction.**

Wisdom

If you were asked to choose between a bag of gold coins and a tablet with words of wisdom, which one would you choose? Most people would go for the gold, and that would be enough. However, the words of wisdom would be the best. If you have wisdom, you can get several bags of gold. If you have bags of gold coins and do not have wisdom, you will end up losing the gold.

Wisdom, by simple definition, is the ability to apply knowledge. Wisdom can also be an acute insight into reality or foresight into the future. It causes you to understand things from a deeper perspective. This positions you to have clarity in life. You always know what to do and how to do it.

Wisdom directs you to say what should be said, do what should be done and think what should be thought. It makes you go where you should go. Wisdom is not passive; it is revealed by action.

When wisdom is working in you, your life will be full of peace. You will not ever have to worry about anything. You will have what they call a good life because of your deeper understanding of things. You will enjoy a journey of peace with prosperity because wisdom will ensure that you have a stress-free life or journey.

Wisdom gives you the insight to acquire and maintain wealth. Without wisdom, when things are acquired, there is a chance you can lose it. For example, it is said that a high percentage of people who won the lottery ended up losing their winnings because they did not have the wisdom to manage their wealth.

Without the function of wisdom, your journey of life can be marked by stress, frustration and disappointment. Wisdom is a priceless tool to help us enjoy life.

Knowledge

A proud, young man once approached Socrates, asking for knowledge. He walked up to the philosopher and said, "O great Socrates, I come to you for knowledge."

Socrates recognised a pompous numbskull when he saw one. He led the young man through the streets, to the sea, and plunged him chest-deep into the water. Then he asked, "What do you want?"

"Knowledge, O wise Socrates," said the young man with a smile.

Socrates put his strong hands on the man's shoulders and pushed him under. Thirty seconds later he let him up. "What do you want?" he asked again.

"Wisdom," the young man sputtered, "O great and wise Socrates!"

Socrates dunked him under again. Thirty seconds passed. Thirty-five. Forty. Socrates let him up. The man was gasping. "What do you want, young man?"

Between heavy, heaving breaths the fellow wheezed, "Knowledge, O wise and wonderful –"

Socrates plunged him under again. Forty seconds passed. Fifty. "What do you want?"

"Air!" the young man screeched. "I need air!"

"When you want knowledge as you have just wanted air, then you will have knowledge."

The story of the young man seeking knowledge from Socrates provides us with an example of how the desire for knowledge must come before we can acquire it. The desire for self-improvement and self-expansion will enrich our inner world, which highlights a prior thought: everything you want in life begins from within you.

Knowledge, according to Merriam-Webster's Dictionary, is *"the fact or condition of being aware of something or knowing something with familiarity gained through experience or association."* It also means *"acquaintance with understanding a science, art, or technique."* Knowledge can also be described as *"the circumstance or condition of apprehending truth or fact through reasoning."*

The world has become very dynamic. We are in the Information Age and experiencing something called 'information overload'. In this Age, you can get information on almost anything you want. This is where the Path of Achievers comes into full force. You must be skilled and intentional to only seek the information that will benefit your future. Achievers acquire the knowledge and skill to help them deal with the challenges they are faced with. Any obstacle you encounter on this journey should be perceived as an opportunity to learn, overcome, and elevate to the next level in life. It is important to note that the knowledge we have is like a grain of sand on the seashore. The information you have is the information you can use. The only thing that limits a person is his ignorance. *Ignorance* is a disease because it is impossible to excel in an area you have no knowledge of.

I remember a couple of years ago, my lack of knowledge about the banking industry cost me a great deal. Almost every month, I incurred unnecessary charges because I was ignorant about the effects of paying my bills late. However, after receiving meaningful financial education, it became easier to save and deal with my finances wisely. Knowledge protects you from unnecessary trouble.

On the Path of Achievers, you have to master the area in which you want to see the most success. You must master your area of interest. The knowledge you gain from mastery will protect, sustain you and cause you to excel in your chosen field.

Knowledge is an integral part of our lives. Each person goes through life learning to live and to adapt to the next environment. We acquire the right knowledge to get the right results from the things that confront us. The difference between an achiever and an under-achiever is what they know. For the achiever, the information they have freely offers them a unique edge in life.

Apply Your Knowledge

To benefit from the knowledge you possess, you must apply it. Most times, when people receive information, they fail to apply it. This could come in the form of reading a book or listening to an audiobook or podcast, but we fail to put the information to use. We have to learn to treasure it and learn to apply it to situations to give us the results we desire. It is not useful to know something and not apply it.

Have you heard the saying *'knowledge is power'*? Well, knowledge only becomes power when it is applied and shared. Moreover, one of the hallmarks of achievers is being able to apply their knowledge to new situations. This means transferring knowledge from one context to another. The application of your knowledge in a small context is limiting. In society, the transfer of knowledge, strategies and techniques occurs daily across various fields of studies. This often leads to new insights and new ways of approaching situations. Knowledge is attractive; the more we know, the more we want to know. As achievers, we need to learn to desire more knowledge to achieve more in our lives.

Instruction

Instruction as a feature of the intellect is your ability to take and receive guidance. Instruction is a direction, order, and systematic procedure. This is an indispensable element in the unfolding of your life as an achiever. Instruction can be taken from various sources. An example of instruction can be seen in mentorship. Mentorship generally is the transference of information. As a person, there are many things that you may not have known or experienced, even though you are on the Path of Achievers. There are some people whom you can learn from as they are at the destination you want to get to. Their achievement has manifested on the outside. Therefore, it is crucial that you carefully choose a mentor. Your future is decided by the person whom you have chosen to listen to and whom to learn from.

Mentors are priceless! They are guides along the path. If you have ever taken a tour of a large metropolitan area, you will understand the importance of a guide.

Let's suppose you take a trip to Dubai. It is your first visit, and you have a guide to show you the popular hotspots and sights. At some point, amid the crowded streets, you become separated from your guide. You take a few turns on your own and find yourself walking down a dark alleyway, which comes to a dead-end. You suddenly realise you are alone, and fear grips your heart.

Likewise, in life, without an experienced guide, you can quickly lose your way and come to that dark, dead-end. You may find various mentors at various points in your life. You must do your best to find a mentor or mentors because they will help unleash your potential and save you from making costly mistakes. They are your coaches and guides. Sir Isaac Newton once said, *"If I have seen further it is by standing on the shoulders of giants."*

In other words, get someone who has "been there, done that." Find a mentor who has done the things you aspire to do and succeeded, because their wisdom is something that can be translated directly into your life in a real, positive way.

IMAGINATION

Imagination is the creative faculty of a person. It is the ability to form new images and sensations when they are not perceived through sight, hearing, or other senses. Of all the creatures on Earth, none can imagine except humans. Your imagination is your creative ability – your arsenal and weapon. You can accomplish great feats with it; overcome great challenges and birth great innovations and solutions. The Wright brothers pioneered aviation and invented the world's first successful airplane – an idea developed first in their imagination.

Napoleon Hill stated: "*Through the aid of his imaginative faculty, man has discovered and harnessed more of nature's forces during the past fifty years than during the entire history of the human race, previous to that time. He has conquered the air so completely that the birds are a poor match for him in flying. He has harnessed the ether, and made it serve as a means of instantaneous communication with any part of the world. He has analysed and weighed the sun at a distance of millions of miles, and has determined, through the aid of IMAGINATION, the elements of which it consists. He has discovered that his own brain is both a broadcasting and a receiving station for the vibration of thought, and he is beginning now to learn how to make practical use of this discovery. He has increased the speed of locomotion, until he may now travel at a speed of more than three hundred miles an hour. The time will soon come when a man may have breakfast in New York and lunch in San Francisco.*"

Imagination is such a powerful faculty in us that it has, over the years, given individuals the opportunity to do tremendous things in life. Education and training are helpful, but they are not the only requirements for success in life. Creative imagination creates a vital role in the lives of an individual. The pages of history are inscribed with uneducated pioneers whose great thoughts allowed them to become masters in their chosen fields.

It was Albert Einstein who said *"Imagination is everything. It is the preview of life's coming attractions."* Walt Disney, using his imagination, created a cartoon character called Mickey Mouse and imagined the theme park, Disneyland. Legions of authors including, J.K. Rowling, attribute their achievements to the power of imagination.

Imagination is the ability to visualise images you want to see in the future, using the eyes of the mind. There is no limit to your value or your capabilities when it comes to the power of your imagination.

There is power for an individual to create whatever they desire. Imagination can give you an idea of the future before you even see the manifestation thereof.

Imagination is the source and centre of all man's creative power. The power that elevates him from brute creation and that gives him dominion from the rest of creation. Some people believed that the imagination was make-believe – the irony. But imagination is directly connected to visualisation. Imagination pictures the things you desire. Vision idealises it. Everything human beings have created and will ever create lies at the centre of his imagination. Majority of the everyday resources we take for granted were imagined. The Internet. Your mobile device. Your clothes. Your bed. As an achiever, by harnessing the power of your imagination, you can create the life you want.

So, you have a gift. Use it! Channel the thoughts, ideas and images that form, develop and animate in your mind into advantageous opportunities to benefit your future. Make them work and produce for you what you desire. It is essential to use your imagination to rework reality and problem-solve things as they could be not as they are or currently appear to be. They should be real, lively and interesting. Do not merely dream but imagine things as you want them to be and for the good of mankind.

Strategies for using the Imagination:

> **1. Give your mind something to work on.** One of the greatest secrets to success is initiative. This is the quality that promotes people. So, conceive something first in your mind as a mental image.
>
> **2. Believe it. Picture it so clearly that you BELIEVE you HAVE it.** The very moment you get hold of your mental image or impression; it becomes a reality. It may be a while before you realise it, but the most critical part is done. You have created the model. However, it is up to you to believe it can manifest.

EMOTIONS

A man was polishing his new car when his six-year-old son picked up a stone and scratched lines on the side panel of the car. Excited, his son called his dad over to show him what he had done. The man looked at the side of his car and in anger, gripped his son's hand vigorously. He was so angry he did not realise his strength. At the hospital, the doctor shared his diagnosis with the child's father; his son suffered internal bleeding in his hand caused by multiple fractures.

When the child saw his father, with painful eyes, he asked, 'Dad, when will my hand get better?'

The man was hurt and speechless. He went back to his car and began to kick it. Devastated by his actions, he looked intently at the scratches. The child had written 'LOVE YOU DAD'.

There are many times when so many of us experience strong emotions. These intense feelings are good, but it is bad to let them overpower you. Most of us, knowingly or unknowingly are susceptible to them. They are linked to situations that are either real or imagined and are based on judgments about the extent that the current situation meets our goals. Emotions play a significant part in our daily lives. Like the father in the story, we sometimes make decisions based on how we are feeling, whether we are happy, angry, sad, bored or frustrated. When you fail to process your emotions and experiences, you create toxins of a sort within yourself. Emotional toxins manifest as anxiety, depression, sadness, hopelessness, anger, rage, impatience, or guilt. At times, we can let our emotions get the better of us. We must rid ourselves of any bad emotions and instead develop a healthy emotional life, which helps us to achieve success in life.

Our ability to manage our emotions well is linked to us achieving success in life. Let's say you are in a leadership position at work. Your ability to handle your emotions is paramount to you succeeding in that position. If you are emotionally charged, constantly getting angry, it will affect your effectiveness as a leader. In relationships, partners who take responsibility for their feelings and manage them well will be more successful at problem-solving and relationship building than those who always blame the other person.

Benefits of Emotions

Emotions appear to serve several physical and psychological purposes. Some scientists believe that emotions are one of the fundamental traits associated with being human.

Emotions colour our lives and give them depth and differentiation. Our emotions provide clues on who we are and how we have been affected and shaped by our past. This is especially true regarding our dominant emotions. Many of our actions are initiated by emotion, which leads naturally to the question: which emotions are being surfaced, and why? We see the world through the lens of our dominant emotions. Emotions are closely linked to creativity and expression — like a musician whose connection to lyrics allows them to perform in front of a live audience with great passion, or an actor who taps into their own emotions to play a character so well that they "become" the character. On a fundamental level, art, music, and literature aim to arouse an emotional response and create an emotional connection between the artist/character and audience/reader.

Physiologically, emotions enable us to adapt to certain situations and curveballs. Emotions help us to survive. They motivate us to act quickly and take actions that will maximise our potential for success. Sudden fear often causes a person to freeze, like a deer caught by a car's headlights. When you feel fear, you are more likely to either freeze or flee. At its simplest level, fear inhibits our decisions to take risks – positive and negative. On the other hand, emotions like anger can instantly activate an external response, such as confronting the person of our irritation.

EMOTIONAL MANAGEMENT

You are responsible for your emotions, and to be an achiever, you need to take charge of your emotions. We need to be keen to face any emotional imbalance or disturbance. For this, it is imperative to understand the active role of emotions in our lives. We need to realise up to what extent we can get control of them. Apply wisdom when dealing with your feelings, and you will achieve tremendous results. Failure to do so can result in embarrassment because of how you handle yourself under pressure. Emotional intelligence is the mark of a true achiever.

Emotions are feelings associated with stimuli, which can be internal or external. The internal and external expressions of stimuli reflect our lives and can impact our success. To become the people that we were born to be, we need to apply ourselves in an environment that promotes a healthy emotional life. People who lead unproductive and fruitless lives have allowed negative emotions to steer their personal journeys. Emotional intelligence is a key component in a healthy emotional life and becoming someone of significance. Emotional management demands you develop emotional intelligence and emotional self-control.

Having Emotional Intelligence

In his award-winning book 'Emotional Intelligence', Psychologist Daniel Goleman examines our ability to monitor our emotional states and use this information to act wisely in wide-ranging relationships. Scientists who study emotions, generally believe that people with high emotional intelligence work well in cooperative situations, and are good at motivating and managing others. People with low emotional intelligence often misinterpret emotional signals and have underdeveloped interpersonal skills. Although emotional intelligence probably has an inherited component, many psychologists believe that people can be guided into making better use of the emotional intelligence that they already possess.

Emotional intelligence includes:
- **Self-awareness** – to recognise internal feelings
- **Managing emotions** – handling emotions in varying situations
- **Motivation** – using self-control to channel emotions toward accomplishing a goal
- **Empathy** – understanding the emotional perspectives of other people
- **Handling relationships** – using privileged information about others to relate better with them.

Having Emotional Self-Control

In another text, *'Emotional Self-Awareness: A Primer'*, Psychologist Daniel Goleman describes emotional self-control as *"the ability to keep your disruptive emotions and impulses in check, to maintain your effectiveness under stressful or even hostile conditions."* Goleman's view does not give permission to suppress your emotions, but instead pay even closer attention to your feelings and accompanying bodily signals, and choose wisely whether to or how to act on them. In other words, to think before you act.

Emotional self-control includes:

- **Using relaxation techniques** – this can be achieved by cultivating hobbies, doing things that please us, inculcating a sense of optimism and positivity, and practising breathing exercises and meditation.
- **Being conscious of what you are feeling** – observe and describe your emotions in a positive and not condemning way.
- **Change the direction of your thoughts.** Behind every emotion is a thought. Changing negative thoughts into positive thoughts (i.e. positive criticism) will tremendously impact your emotional output. You can choose to have positive emotions.

Protecting your emotional life is pivotal to guarding what enters your inner world. Do not underestimate the power of your emotions and neither be fearful of this power, as emotions can produce or trigger positive motion towards your goals in life. Starting today, take back control of your emotions. One of the strategies in enriching our inner world is choosing to be happy. Happiness is a state of mind and has nothing to do with external influences. When we feel balanced inside, it will enhance our performance outside.

WILL

Your will helps you to make quintessential choices. Your will is evidenced by statements like *"I will go to..."*, *"I will make sure..."*, *"I will.."*, *"we will..."*. They suggest a personal want, determination, and desire to do something. Self-determination powered by your will is fundamental because your pathway to achievement is motivated by your will. Your will suggests that you can control your impulses or instincts. Self-control and self-mastery are by-products of your will.

The will is what one wishes or has determined shall be accomplished. It is the motive behind a person's action. Choice is more directional than a wish. In fact, choice is the immediate cause of all actions. Choice implies the rejection of one thing and the acceptance of an alternative, whether it be positive or negative. In every act of will, there is a preference, desiring one thing rather than another. Where there is no preference, but complete indifference, there is no choice or volition.

To will is to choose, and to choose is to decide between two or more alternatives. This could be a relatively simple choice of what to wear on a special occasion. For more complex decisions, we might need further support to help in the decision-making process.

The will is the power that helps us to persevere long after the decision is made. However, not everyone can follow his or her decision through. For example, someone can decide, with the best intentions, to quit smoking, but after some time may succumb to the craving.

What makes people go back on a decision? Lack of self-control? Lack of self-discipline? Or are they just too weak to carry on? Well, those are legitimate questions to consider. From my coaching experience over the years, I have observed that most people have issues with self-control, which led me to develop solution-based programmes that my mentees have found very useful. Let's explore the role that strong will play in having self-control.

I believe that your personal willpower is inextricably linked to whether or not your resolve can endure. Willpower makes all the difference in the world. It is the force behind most success stories. Willpower helps build new habits and is what keeps achievers on their chosen course, no matter how difficult the journey gets. It allows people to resist distraction or temptation and helps them to continue to lead a productive lifestyle. For example, a person with a weak will often decides, with the same good intention as one with a strong will, to do something. Still, after a lapse of time, his or her motivation to carry out a decision does not persist, because of a lack of willpower.

Though there is some controversy around willpower, research suggests that it should be considered as if it were a muscle. This indicates that we can make our willpower stronger as we make our muscles stronger. To strengthen a muscle, you have to exercise, and when you overwork a muscle, it becomes tiring and recovery time is needed. Putting this into the context of self-control means we can train our willpower consistently but should rest from time to time so our "willpower muscle" has a chance to restore its energy levels.

Willpower Management

Imagine you have just opened the fridge. Inside, there is a big slice of cake in front of you. It looks delightful and delicious. You cannot resist the temptation. You give in to your impulses and eat the cake. As you finish it, you have feelings of regret and anger with your lack of willpower.

Interestingly, there are several variables to deal with daily as we journey on the Path of Achievers. Willpower has been proven to play a major role in our achievements in life. As a result, I have proposed what I call 'Willpower Management'. This is the process of empowering your will so that it can serve you effectively as you journey in life. Like a muscle, you can strengthen your willpower with frequent use. The underlying mechanism of 'Willpower Management' is simply learning how to control your attention and thoughts. This includes self-knowledge, meditation, exercise, rest and stress management.

Self-Knowledge

The first step towards strengthening your willpower is to be aware of your strengths and weaknesses. When you begin your journey of self-knowledge, there are things you can learn about yourself. Among them are your temperament, capabilities, expertise – and personal values.

Daniel Goleman proposed self-awareness as *"knowing one's internal states, preference, resources and intuitions."* And as stated by Dr Kelly McGonigal, author of 'Willpower Instinct', *"to succeed at self-control, you need to know how you fail."* It is also about knowing your trigger points, your mental traps and your habits. You can use the questions below to evaluate yourself.

Where do you most often 'give in'?

When do you most often 'give up'?

What exhausts your willpower the most?

Meditation

Meditation is focusing your attention on a chosen thought or activity for a determined time while resisting the urge to drift. A simple meditation practice that can be applied is 'mindfulness' – focusing your attention on what is happening in the present, including your external environment, internal thoughts, and so on. I can assure you that after 2-3 days of meditation for 10 minutes, you can focus better, have more energy, and you will be less stressed.

Start with approximately 10 minutes of mindfulness, in a quiet place focusing particularly on your breathing. When we practise 'mindful meditation', we are also engaging the prefrontal cortex, a part of our brain that regulates our emotions and decision-making and thus, can boost our willpower. Focusing on this will prove most effective compared to letting our impulses take over. Meditation provides fast results for strengthening willpower due to its power and ability to build self-awareness and control our impulses.

Exercise Daily

Ten minutes of exercise daily can boost your willpower immensely. The strategy is to start small and build up the amount of exercise you do until you have more control, increasing the amount of time as your willpower improves. This is key, especially if you are not used to or loathe exercising. For example, you can start by walking for 10 minutes and increase intensity – and duration – over time as your willpower improves. It is well-known that people who promise to exercise daily but do not, are inhibited by a lack of self-discipline. Lack of self-discipline is an outcome of underdeveloped willpower.

Sleep Well

Research shows that adequate rest improves our self-control and provides the best environment for the brain to function. When you rest, it reduces the body's need for glucose, allowing the body to make use of what it has. Adequate rest is generally 7-8 hours a night for an adult, and 10-12 hours a night for a child.

Stress Management

According to research, behaviour is influenced when the 'fight-or-flight' response is triggered. The connection between stress and willpower impacts this biochemical signal. When we are relaxed, we are more likely to listen to the rational part of our brain, instead of acting emotionally and yielding to temptations.

As stated by Dr Kelly McGonigal in her ground-breaking book, *Willpower Instinct*, we need to manage our stress levels. Increased stress requires increased energy from your body to act instinctively and make decisions based on short-term outcomes. In effect, you are depleting your body of much-needed energy. In highly stressful scenarios, your prefrontal cortex loses out in the battle for energy.

Dr McGonigal proposes that we should stop to take a few deep breaths when we feel overwhelmed or tempted. This will kick-start the process of managing your stress levels and improving your willpower.

In conclusion, the will is the want and desire to accomplish a goal. Your willingness to be an achiever influences your ability to do the things that will make you an achiever. You must be strong-willed on the Path of Achievers, especially when you determine in your mind to accomplish something. You must be willing to do everything in your power, to achieve what you want.

REFLECTION

| REFLECTION |

CHAPTER SEVEN

Living Effectively

Effective living suggests living out your maximum potential. It is the result of living from the inside out and requires that you tap into your flow, which is your optimal state of consciousness. Your flow is elevated when you live effectively: living out your life's purpose, which gives you an innate reason for living. In light of this, you must understand the mechanism of living effectively, which is based on the principle of Living from the Inside Out. This fundamental law in creation reveals that we can attract our desired realities by what we think or say. This is the achiever's principle. You can be anything you want to be, get anything you want to get and do anything you want to do: if you dedicate yourself to these principles and life truths. You can control the things around you, including the circumstances in your life. They can help you deal wisely with the affairs of life, rule and subdue your environment. Watch as you become an agent for change, a life-giver and an achiever.

An Introduction to the Achiever's Principle

The Achiever's Principle is the creative principle that helps you create the life you want and desire. By observing and applying this principle, you will become the achiever you were born to be. This principle gives birth to the understanding that your outer world is a reflection of your inner world. We will be unpacking the achiever's principle in more depth later on in the text.

Understanding the Principle of 'Living From the Inside Out'

People tend to gain their self-worth 'from the outside in'. Their worth tends to be dependent on the material possessions that they have acquired, or the status or pedigree given to them by society. For example, someone may purchase a brand-new car and automatically believe that they are more important than others.

When we are driven by the desire to own expensive goods, we will never be satisfied or fulfilled. Some people spend their lives striving for this and end up indulging in all kinds of acts and vices. Some sell drugs or commit other crimes to get the money to live the materialistic lifestyle they want. This unfortunate mindset is not applicable to every person. There are people living authentically; earning finances legitimately. However, the fact remains that people still approach life from the standpoint of 'outside in.' This problematic approach to life creates undue challenges. For example, have you worn your clothes inside out without noticing before? Until someone tells you, you remain completely unaware of this faux pas. And so it is with life itself sometimes. We sometimes live a certain way and do not realise what we are doing until someone points it out to us.

In most cases, we pick our model for living from our parents or society. Social systems and infrastructures teach us how to live in the outer world. Whereas, in reality, schools fail to train us for the 'real world', including the realities of the working world. While we are taught about the wonders of the world through subjects such as history, geography, biology and mathematics; we cannot solely exist and thrive successfully through the lens of biology, chemistry, and mathematics. We must equally learn about the importance of our inner world. Inasmuch as the knowledge we gain from understanding the world and how it works is great, it would be extremely valuable to take an equal-weighted approach to understand how our inner world works. There is no core subject, course or curriculum out there that trains you on the discipline of understanding and harnessing your inner world to impact your outer world. While we may witness pockets of this concept at schools etc, a disproportionate amount of emphasis is placed on the greater value of the outer world. In my opinion, our inner world is of incomparable significance.

People who understand themselves, live from the inside out. When you understand your true self, you will see that the beauty of YOU is within YOU, which helps you live authentically. The principle of living from the inside out is not exclusive to the minds of prominent teachers and the sacred texts, but we also see it reflected in nature and science.

Every tree has heartwood at its centre; every organic system evolves from the inside out. All species share in the awe-inspiring design of this magnificent universe. Living from the inside out is living from the knowledge of you. It simply means: look within, listen, and live from your centre.

When you are living 'from the outside in'...
- You measure your self-worth by the approval of others or by material possessions.
- You measure your success by the magnitude of your external achievements.
- You are constantly trying to prove yourself by comparing yourself to others.
- You believe that the outside world is the real world, and you relate to it that way.
- You are constantly trying to and searching for happiness out there.
- You are either worrying about the future or living in the past.
- You generally have mostly negative emotions because of mundane, everyday events.
- You feel unsure about who you are because you are trying to live out the opinions of others about you.

When you are living 'from the inside out'...
- You have an innate reason for living.
- You choose to love and accept yourself and do away with the external need for approval or validation.
- You are grounded and accepting of others.

- Your thoughts and actions are expressions of an inner sense of your identity, purpose and intentions rather than simply being reactions to outer circumstances and events.
- You experience a steady state of well-being rather than an unstable and unsure life.
- You can see the end from the beginning and are working your way closer to your destination.
- You experience inner serenity and harmony in your life.
- You live authentically.
- You have an internal locus of control, and you control the events of your life rather than a barrage of random happenings.
- You are in charge of your affairs.

CONSCIOUSNESS

Consciousness is awareness of oneself in the world, of your own inner state and the events going on around you. It can also be viewed as awareness of your unique thoughts, memories, feelings, sensations, and environment. Your consciousness is your awareness of yourself and the world around you. This awareness is subjective and unique to you; it defines you. Simply put, your consciousness is the sum of who you are.

Your consciousness is continually shifting and changing. For example, one moment, you may be focused on reading this book. Your consciousness may then shift to a memory of a conversation you had earlier with someone. Next, you might notice how uncomfortable you are on your chair or your bed, or maybe you catch yourself daydreaming of planning an event. This ever-shifting stream of thoughts can change markedly from one moment to the next, but your experience of it seems smooth and effortless.

There have been a lot of deliberations on consciousness in all the major fields. American psychologist William James compared consciousness to a stream, unbroken and continuous despite constant shifts and changes. Psychoanalyst Sigmund Freud focused on understanding the importance of the unconscious and conscious mind. It is about dealing with the world out there; your environment, and the world within; your consciousness. Some different states of consciousness include sleep, dreams, hypnosis, hallucinations, meditation, and the effects of psychoactive drugs.

Your consciousness can define you and influence your life. Living life from the inside out means living from your consciousness. Having knowledge or the understanding of certain secrets or laws of life gives you an edge in society. Consciousness can be linked to your mindset, as well. There is an optimal state which allows you to be effective in life. A significant number of sports personalities, musicians, entrepreneurs, scientists and others discovered this high state of consciousness and used it to produce peak performances when it mattered. This is termed differently. Some call it their "flow", others "being in your zone", others call it "revelation". Whatever the name, there is a state that we enter, which enables us to be at our best. These are mechanisms within us, hence the principle of 'living from the inside out.' As this discussion progresses, you have to understand that to be effective as an individual is your personal responsibility and is something that is within your control. You can choose to live effectively and always bring out your best.

INNER LIFE

The thought of the inner life excites me. When we talk of the inner life, we are talking about the environment within you. In life, our real environment is the one within us, the life of the inner self, and how we live that out. We can consciously programme our inner world to enhance our outer life. It is a fact that anything that happens outside us or in our lives begins from within us. Ancient Greek Historian and Philosopher Plutarch stated: *"What we achieve inwardly will change outer reality."* Things are created twice, first within us, then manifested outside. In essence, you create the blueprint first. We create the kind of lives we want by first creating it inside us. Achievement in life begins with achievement within. In other words, to achieve anything on the outside, we must first achieve it on the inside.

By realising the life in our inner world and enriching our inner world, we will possess harmony, serenity and balance, which enhance our outer world and our effectiveness on the outside. Whatever we accommodate on the inside always reflects on the outside. For example, sometimes when we fear that something will happen, by the time it does, we realise that, that fear has manifested on the outside. When we come to have a full understanding of this concept, we will create the lives we want and deserve.

Inner life means being in touch with your fundamental self. The vast terrain of your hopes and dreams, thoughts, emotions, love, dedication, devotion, compassion, care and concern – and intuition – are very vital instincts. It is a private space for imagining and reflecting which nourishes you and gives you a sense of well-being. Each one of us has an outer life and an inner life. Our outer life is our contact with the physical world and is filled with material comfort. This is not satisfying unless you also enjoy an abundantly rich inner life, filled with meaning and purpose. The inner life draws its source and vitality from your inner world. This once again includes your mind, will, and emotions, which foundationally, create and shape your view of your outer life.

Intuition

Your intuition is a great sense within you. Understanding the importance of it and using it can create tremendous benefits in your life. Intuition is a process that gives us the ability to know something directly and instinctively without analytic or conscious reasoning, bridging the gap between the conscious and non-conscious parts of our mind, between instincts and reasoning.

Steve Jobs once said that intuition is *"more powerful than intellect."*

Your instinct is an innate ability, and everyone has it. Without instinct, we will be just like a computer, acting and doing everything based on binary code. The more you listen to your intuition, and the more you follow it, the more powerful it can be. It is like a muscle; with practise, you can train your intuition to grow stronger. You must follow your intuition and your heart. It is difficult to hear your inner voice sometimes, and this is especially true for people who think more logically. Sometimes, you just have to listen to your gut feeling.

Jobs also advised: "... *and most important, have the courage to follow your heart and intuition. They somehow already know what you truly want to become. Everything else is secondary.*"

Listening to your intuition is listening to your inner voice (your gut feeling), to understand your feelings and hear your inner wisdom.

Programming Your Inner World

As our inner world affects our outer reality, in the same way, our lifestyles and habits have a profound effect on our inner world. Our inner world is like a fertile garden; it grows the seeds we plant in there. In the context of our discussion, I will relate our inner world to *the mind*. If we cultivate our inner world with care, we will experience a deep sense of peace and inner serenity. We can programme the mind to have the desired character we want. **There are simple practises that can help you gain increased control over your inner experience; practising these exercises will help expand or enrich your consciousness.**

Programming Your Mind

The mind is like a fertile, rich garden. If you care for it, nurture it and cultivate it, it will blossom far beyond your expectations. As a result, lasting peace of mind and deep inner harmony will be yours. We have to guard the gates of our mind against toxic waste each day. Worries and anxieties, unnecessary fears and disturbance of peace should not enter these gates. Our ability to live in the two worlds successfully is what makes us achievers in life. In essence, what really separates achievers and under-achievers is how the circumstances of their lives are interpreted and processed. Achievers see the positive side of everything that happens in their lives. They are optimistic and have the right perspective of life, and therefore they live life in a higher dimension. Their worldview came as a result of their desire to train themselves to perceive the world in a more positive way. Achievers are able to sow good seeds in the fertile garden of their minds with the way they interpret and process the events outside of them. One of the practical ways to guard your mind is by controlling the thoughts you dwell on. You cannot stop a bird from flying over your head, but you can stop it from perching on your head. Inasmuch as thoughts and ideas come to your mind, you have to choose not to dwell on them. As you continually do that, you will gain more mastery in controlling your mind and thereby controlling your actions and reactions.

Fill your mind with peaceful experiences. You must learn that the easiest way to a peaceful mind is to keep your mind in a peaceful state. This is done by practise and by the application of some simple techniques outlined in this book. The mind responds to teaching and discipline so you can reap the benefits of the positive outcome you have conditioned it for. The mind can only give back what was first given.

Condition your mind with peaceful words and ideas, and ultimately you will have a reservoir of peace – producing experiences to which you may turn for refreshment and renewal of yourself. It will be a vast source of power. We live in a day and age where everything is done at a fast pace. We have become so impatient and want everything now! This habit has made us lose our peace of mind, and we are not always able to calm down, relax or concentrate effectively on the task at hand.

To control the mind, you can practise the exercises outlined in the next secton. They will help you gain more control and power over yourself and the events of your life. Just try them for 21 days, (three full weeks). As a result, you will enrich your inner world, and therefore, enhance your outer world and be more effective in anything you do.

ENRICHING YOUR CONSCIOUSNESS

MEJ is the acronym for **Meditation, Exercising and Journaling**. Over the years, I have mentored and worked with diverse groups of people, and I have found that this model is an effective tool for expanding one's awareness of self and their environment.

Meditation

Meditation is one of the techniques to programme the mind as well as help your desires materialise. Meditation is focusing your attention on something for a definite period. It brings you into the present, focusing on emotions, thoughts, and sensations that you are experiencing 'in the now.' While it can be initially difficult to quieten your thoughts, with time and practise, you can experience the benefits of mindfulness meditation, including less stress and anxiety, and even a reduction in physical symptoms. This exercise has a way of calming you down and crystallising your goals in life.

If you are new to meditation, you will find the following guidelines useful:

- Find a quiet and comfortable place. Sit in a place where you are not stiff. It is also helpful to wear comfortable clothing, so you are not distracted.
- Try to put aside all thoughts of the past and the future and focus on the present.
- Become aware of your breath, attuning to the sensation of air moving in and out of your body as you breathe. Pay attention to the way each breath changes and is different.
- Watch every thought come and go, whether it is a worry, fear, anxiety, or hope. When thoughts come up in your mind, do not ignore or suppress them. Simply note them, remain calm, and use your breathing as an anchor.
- If you find yourself getting carried away in your thoughts, observe where your mind went off to without judgment, and return to your breathing exercises. Remember not to be hard on yourself if this happens.

- As the time comes to a close, sit for a minute or two, becoming aware of where you are. Get up with conviction knowing you have attained inner balance.

Exercise

Exercising is an effective way to enrich your consciousness. Exercise is any bodily activity that enhances or maintains physical fitness and overall health and wellness. When you are exercising, you are focused on the activity that takes you to an expanded conscious state as well as keeping your physical body fit. There are so many exercise programmes you can join if you are a beginner. I enjoy jogging, which produces excellent benefits for my mental, physical and emotional well-being. Doing some basic exercises – running, walking, dancing, or any other activities – helps to raise the endorphin levels in your brain, increasing your circulation, which makes you feel more empowered. Physical activity is one of the greatest ways to help the brain settle into stillness and reconnect with the heart to align with what matters most in your life.

Journaling

Journaling is the practice of keeping a journal that explores thoughts and feelings surrounding the events of your life. There are several different ways to do this. Journaling, as a self-exploration tool, works best when done consistently. It can be a great way to document your thoughts and awareness, which helps you to track your consciousness over a period of time. When the practice is focused on gratitude or emotional processing, it can be a soothing activity on your subconscious because you are allowing your mind to release thoughts that you would normally ignore throughout the day. This activity helps record your special memories, as well as locating yourself, and it is a great tool for self-awareness. I have been journaling for many years. It has helped me stay focused. When I go through my journals, it reminds me of things I ought to do. I have also recommended this to my clients, and it has been such a helpful tool for them too.

When we live from the inside out, especially when our inner world is enriched, it automatically propels our effectiveness on the outside. Being effective is the desire of everyone because it makes us come alive and gets all our juices flowing. I have found that observing the principle of living from the inside out guarantees your effectiveness in life.

REFLECTION

CHAPTER EIGHT

Creative Living

Your future is not ahead of you,
it's trapped within you.
– Myles Munroe

Creative living is living by design and not by default. It means being intentional about your life and designing your future from the inside out. This way of living gives you control of your life and brings fulfilment. On the contrary, living by default is living in autopilot mode. In a recent study of 3,000 people living in the UK, led by Professor Renata Salecl and Dr Mark Williamson, 96% of them admitted to living life on autopilot. The researchers concluded that as our lives have become more frantic, and we are increasingly overwhelmed, autopilot has become our default mode. It has led to an epidemic of subconscious decision-making, with the average person making 15 mindless decisions every day - 250,000 autopilot decisions over a lifetime.

I firmly believe that we can design our future because our future is trapped within us, just as the future of a seed is within the seed. The future of an apple seed is within itself, that is, to become an apple tree, in the same way, our future is within us. It is your responsibility to design the future that you want instead of leaving it to chance. This makes you live by design instead of by default – the essence of creative living.

Living your life by design requires you to actively take a practical approach in the investment of your future. For example, write down your vision, set time to set your goals, and map out plans of how you can reach your desired destination. A model that you might find useful in helping you to live by design is the **VAQ model**. The model allows individuals to actualise their goals. **'VAQ'** is an acronym for **Visualisation, Affirmation and Quiet time**.

VISUALISATION

Visualisation is the technique for creating images, diagrams, or animations to communicate a message. Visualisation, through visual imagery, has been an effective way to communicate both abstract and concrete ideas since the dawn of time. In essence, there is a natural law of cause and effect, which makes the dream of the dreamer come true. It is the law of visualisation – the law that calls into being in this outer material world, everything that is real in the inner world. Examples from history include cave paintings, Egyptian hieroglyphics, Greek geometry, and Leonardo da Vinci's revolutionary methods of technical drawing for engineering and scientific purposes. Visualisation will help your personal growth and assist you in every way. It is the power to create the outcome you desire based on the ageless principle that everything is created twice: first in the mind, then in reality. This technique is highly effective in manifesting your desires. It will work for everyone: the student who wants to get better grades at school or the business professional who wants to attract lucrative contracts and opportunities.

The technique is 'The Mirror Principle', which envisions your dreams becoming a reality. The mind works through pictures. Pictures affect your self-image, and self-image affects the way you feel, act and achieve. If your self-image tells you that you are too young to change your habits for the better, you will never change for the better. If your self-image tells you that you do not deserve a higher life, this will ultimately become your reality. But when you visualise inspiring pictures through the film of your mind, wonderful things start to happen in your life. If you spend time every day, even just a few minutes, in the practice of creative envisioning and seeing yourself as you want to be, you will eventually fulfil your desires.

Creative visualisation, just like natural laws, works for everyone. What is important to remember at this point is that, whether or not you are consciously aware of it, you are continuously visualising and creating what you see in your physical world, through your mind. The majority of people in the world are not conscious of what they are creating. Most are unconsciously creating the daily events, conditions, and circumstances that they come to experience in their lives and are not even aware of it. This is because your outside environment is a reflection of the environment within you.

It starts in the form of thoughts. Those thoughts are causing you to visualise, (through words, pictures, or feelings) either consciously or unconsciously, the events and circumstances that you see and experience in your life daily. Your creative visualisation is attracting and constantly creating, whether you are aware of it or not. You must become more self-aware of your thoughts; consciously visualise and begin to create the things you desire instead of leaving it to chance to unconsciously create what you do not want in your life. Absolutely nothing in our world can grow without planting a seed first. It is against all scientific and natural laws.

Your thoughts represent the seed to the beliefs you hold. The combination of those thoughts and beliefs are the ingredients, which determine your emotions. Your creative visualisation and affirmations represent the nurturing of that seed. Depending on the specific seeds that you are planting and how you are nurturing those seeds, you determine what you will come to see and experience in your physical world, regardless of if you are doing it consciously or unconsciously.

That law applies to everything in life. There is nothing you can rightfully desire that cannot be brought into being through visualisation. For example, if you want a laptop for work purposes, you can receive it through this power. Imprint the picture of you holding your new work laptop into your mind. See it! Believe it! In time, it will manifest on the outside.

Visualisation is one of the techniques you can use to cause what is inside you (your desires) to manifest on the outside and also to get what you want in life.

How it works

Visualisation is a mental rehearsal. You create images in your mind of having or doing whatever it is that you want. You then repeat these images daily for about five minutes a day. In your five-minute sessions, use your imagination to be successful in whatever goal you may have. *What you focus on, you attract.*

Visualisation is not only on a metaphysical exercise, as some people propose. Research states that athletes have been using it for decades to improve their performance. An article in *Psychology Today* reported that the brain patterns activated when a weightlifter lifts heavy weights are also similarly activated when the lifter just imagines lifting weights. Our brain is an astonishing organ that works toward making us successful with every action we take. Generally, our brains train our bodies to prepare for action. When we imagine ourselves preparing for an activity, our brains run through the process and send signals to the rest of our body to complete the action. So, there is substantial evidence of brain-body connection that affirms the exercise of visualisation as also scientific.

The key to visualising, as John Kehoe suggests in 'Mind Power into the 21st Century', is to always visualise that you already have what you desire. This is a mental trick. Rather than hoping you will achieve it or building confidence that one day it will happen, live and feel it as if it is happening to you now. On one level, you know this is just a mental trick, but the subconscious mind cannot distinguish between what is real and what is imagined. Your subconscious will act upon the images you create within, whether they reflect your current reality or not.

Kehoe has taught this skill to millions of people worldwide, and they have seen the results for themselves. It is not magic, and it does not happen overnight, but if you persist in your vision, you will be successful.

Whatever your definition of success is, you can achieve it. You can achieve anything you put your mind to, once you understand the power of your mind.

Techniques for Visualising

In our attempt to get the things we desire, we sometimes do not know what to do or how to manifest our desires. Well, here are some simple strategies that will help you manifest your desires in life.

The first and most essential strategy is to know that one thing you desire. You need to know what you want before you can focus on getting it. This seems paradoxical, but few people do know what they really want. What is that one thing you want to achieve? You must name it.

Secondly, you must fix in your mind's eye what it is you want. When you consciously keep in your mind precisely what you want by way of visualising, you will manifest your desires.

Know what you want.

Realise that you have the power.

Centre your thoughts upon it with definite purpose.

Vision Boards

To aid with your visualisation process, you can create a vision board.

A vision board is also known as a dream board. It is a physical board documented with the words and pictures that represent your goals and dreams. It serves as a personal notification. It is a tool to aid with your visualisation process, as you seek to create the life you want and achieve your desires. It narrows down your desires and helps you to invest time and energy into visualising your future daily and reminds you of your goals in life. It is a great tool to help turn your dreams into reality. Your vision board must be visible to you to help keep your mind constantly on your goals every day. By the law of attraction, you magnetise and attract to you the people, resources, and opportunities you need to achieve your goal.

AFFIRMATION

According to the English American Dictionary, to 'affirm' is *to state that something is true.*

Affirmations are dynamic and practical.

Your life circumstances are influenced, daily, by the words that you speak. If you are consistently using affirmations of wealth and good fortune, you will experience that in your life in time. Therefore, it is important to say positive things about your life — present and future. In the life of an achiever, your thoughts become your words; and then your words become your actions; actions form into habits; habits become character; then character shapes your destiny. Up to this point, you have learned that you must pay attention to your thoughts because ultimately, you will demonstrate what is always on your mind and become whatever is dominant on your mind.

Your thoughts form your words. What is in you is what comes out as your words. Your words shape your future because they have creative abilities and energy that can chart your course of life. If you continually use negative words to a child, there is a high probability that your words will manifest in the child's life — a self-fulfilling prophecy.

EXERCISE 1

During your visualisation exercise, take your goals and speak them out. For example, think about the desired grade you would like to achieve. You can say something along the lines of, "I am an A* student. The work I produce is A* quality. I receive A*s in all my subjects." If you say this with an internal conviction and belief, it will be yours in no time.

QUIET TIME

Quiet time crystallises your ideas and unleashes your creative energy. Chinese Philosopher Lao Tzu once said, *"Silence is a source of great strength."* Quiet time is an exercise, which suggests spending time alone. With the internet, social media, school, work, taking care of family and loved ones, busy streets, loud noises, things are more chaotic than ever. Most people do not even know what it means to experience 'quiet time'. Some people are always doing something, or wanting to be around others, or watching television - always searching for something to engage them rather than being left alone with their thoughts. The truth is, if you cannot stand yourself, then you cannot stand anyone. Practising quiet time is about being silent and spending time with your thoughts, preferably in solitude. Practising quiet time has enormous benefits such as helping you to be aware of yourself and your environment, unleashing your creative genius, and generating innate power and ability.

EXERCISE 2

Quiet time is the practice of being quiet for a while. Set aside 30 minutes each day — in the early hours of the morning, if that suits — to spend in silence. During this time '**quiet your mind**.' The result of this exercise is to harness the potentialities of the mind. At this point, think of nothing and be in the silent theatre of your mind. Close your eyes then rotate the eyeball upward, far enough to cause a slight strain on the muscles around the eyes. This points the inner vision toward the forehead; then focuses it on the black inner screen. Keep your attention in this manner, and whenever your mind wanders, redirect and start again. Continue this practise until you can sense your inner self and awaken the inner consciousness of quietness, tranquillity, and harmony.

The first few days of practising this exercise might prove difficult, but if you persevere for 21 days, you will begin to enjoy inner serenity and balance. This will significantly enhance your performance on the outside and increase your effectiveness. It can help you to connect with yourself and the power of your mind to awaken the exceptional abilities within you.

EXERCISE 3

Another great 'quiet time' technique is taking a walk. You can walk in silent contemplation focusing on enjoying the vitality and beauty of the nature around you. Listen intently to the quiet sound of nature, and notice its harmonious disposition. The more you observe nature's beauty, the more you enjoy the benefits of bliss.

Daily quiet time will develop your concentration and teach your mind to be still and calm. You will gain tranquillity in your life and your mind. You will feel more vitalised and energised. The elements of worry and imbalances in your life will lose their efficacy and strength.

EXERCISE 4

Draw a black dot (about a quarter of an inch in diameter) on a sheet of paper and stick it to the wall or place it on the floor in front of you. Sit down comfortably, breathing slowly. Stare at this dot and try not to blink. After a while, your eyes will begin to itch. Close your eyes and open them again. Start over.

Do not worry – this exercise will not harm your eyes. On the contrary, it will strengthen the optic nerve and can even help some eye disorders. Start by spending two or three minutes on this exercise, gradually increasing the time. By the end of the first week, you should have reached five minutes. When you have reached 20 minutes, your concentration will be excellent. Repeat some of your favourite affirmations to occupy your thoughts during this exercise.

EXERCISE 5

In the Classic book the power of positive thinking, Vincent Peale Norman recommended the following technique for practising quiet time;

1. Sit relaxed in a chair. Completely yield your body to the chair. Starting with your toes and proceeding to the top of your head, think of every portion of the body as relaxed. Affirm relaxation by saying, "My toes are relaxed... My fingers are relaxed... My facial muscles are relaxed."

the chair. Starting with your toes and proceeding to the top of your head, think of every portion of the body as relaxed. Affirm relaxation by saying, "My toes are relaxed... My fingers are relaxed... My facial muscles are relaxed."

2. Think of your mind as the surface of a lake in a storm, tossed by waves and in tumult. But now the waves have subsided, and the surface of the lake is still and unruffled.

3. Spend two or three minutes thinking of the most beautiful and peaceful scenes you have ever seen such as a mountain with sunset views, a deep valley filled with the hush of the early morning, a wooded area at noonday, or the reflection of the moon on rippling waters. In memory, relive these scenes.

4. Repeat slowly, quietly activating the sound in each of these words which express quietness, i.e. *Tranquility*... Serenity... Peace... Think of other words and repeat them.

5. Make a mental list of times in your life when you have been conscious of God's watchful care and recall how, when you were worried and anxious, He brought things right and took care of you. Then recite aloud this line from an old hymn, "So long thy power hath kept me, sure it STILL will lead me on."

6. Repeat the following, which has an amazing power to relax and quiet the mind: "thou wilt keep him in perfect peace, whose mind is stayed on thee." (Isaiah 26:3) Repeat this several times during the day, whenever you have a fraction of a moment. Repeat it aloud if possible, so that by the end of the day you will have said it many times. Conceive of these words as active, vital substances permeating your mind.

By practising the above exercises, you are intentional and deliberate in creating the life you want.

REFLECTION

CHAPTER NINE

Secret of Achievers

Achieving A Desired Goal – Getting What You Want – Achieving Success In Life. We were all born and designed to be achievers. We have the internal mechanism that it requires. It started from our very conception when you won the race in arriving at the egg before the others. You are a winner from birth. However, when we are born into society, things sometimes appear different. You are cultured into becoming what society wants you to be instead of being the achiever you were born to be. All of us are born in and shaped by the rules and norms of society. Our circumstances do not dictate how successful we become, but it is worth noting that societal conditioning has a significant impact on how we think and see things from an early age. Eventually, we succumb to societal pressures and subscribe to societal definitions and norms, which can create challenges. For example, our society measures success by the externalities of life, such as how grandiose one's house is, designer clothes, the amount of money in your bank account, and many other material things. While these things are good, they do not determine how successful a person is. There are many people who are materially rich but still feel empty, unsatisfied or unfulfilled.

Interestingly, there are a lot of people who primarily define themselves by their material possessions. They pride themselves in their material wealth, which makes them feel important, and their lives more valuable than others. Yet, somewhere along the line, some end up feeling depressed and empty. There are people who have committed suicide because they felt empty and depressed, and leaving behind mansions, cars and wealth. While I have nothing against having material possessions, it is for these reasons and more, that I question the conventional definition of success.

This questioning is evermore necessary when it comes to the lives of young people. We must equip young people to redefine the meaning of success; not from the conventional standpoint of chasing after things which result in stress, depression, crime and many more negatives, but to see success in the light of purpose. True success is the fulfilment of purpose. It is innate, deep. Success 'from the inside out' is the surest and safest place to start. Everything you want in life begins from within you.

Success is from within, not from without

Success is from within and not from without. The secret of success is knowing and realising that you are already a success. You attain success inside of you first before you can attain it on the outside. We have been trained and made to believe that we have to chase success. Success is not a destination but a process. It starts from within you. By extension, everything you want in life begins from within you. This idea ensures that you have a deep inner awareness of what you want to do. It is directly linked to purpose, which is your reason for being. Simon Sinek, author of *'Start with Why'*, shared a very enlightening story.

"I went to an event for high-performing entrepreneurs and the question was asked of the room, 'How many of you have achieved your financial goals?' Amazingly, 80% of the room raised their hand. Then the question was asked, 'How many of you feel successful?' and 80% of the hands went down. This example alone shows that there is little to no connection between the standard measurement of success and the feeling of success."

Whether it is a career you are trying to pursue, or a business idea you have, they will not necessarily make you fulfilled or satisfied until you become more aware of how you are wired, and connect with who you really are.

So, before you do all the outer work to try and change your circumstances, start with the necessary *inner work* to change your inner world. Success within is first based on the principle of living from the inside out and not outside in. Success is a manifestation of an inward conviction. Extract an innate reason, produced from the core of your being, to change your outer reality.

Success Patterns

We all have patterns. These patterns reveal a system that we have created consciously or unconsciously. In the study of success, there is a silver lining or thread, which runs through all of those who have manifested their personal success. It is worth observing and noting these patterns of success to implement them in your life and manifest your success in life. Success patterns are formed or built inside of us and are manifested or realised on the outside.

Just as a wine presser will extract wine from grapes, there are principles and habits that a young achiever ought to develop and cultivate to bring out the success within. To reflect the success within, you must observe certain laws and principles of success. These are patterns because all the people who applied these principles and laws have manifested the success they saw on the inside. Basically, there are repeated success factors that achievers often reference when they speak of their journeys.

Build the patterns you want to see first on the inside, and it will show on the outside. When an architect constructs a building, he first develops the blueprint of the structure. Before the structure is erected, it is already finished on paper. Realising success is the same phenomenon. You must construct the blueprint of the structure on the inside first for it to show on the outside. The good news is that the patterns we need to manifest our personal success are accessible to all of us.

Here are ten success patterns from highly successful people you should adopt to put yourself on the Path of Achievers.

SELF-DISCOVERY

Self-discovery is a prevalent principle in the life of many achievers. They take time to learn about themselves, to discover their strengths and weaknesses. When you take time to know yourself, it comes in handy because we are in an age where a lot of people do not know who they are and what their assignment on Earth is. When you truly discover your real self and understand your real assignment on Earth - you learn that you are powerful beyond measure.

The American English Dictionary defines self-discovery as *"becoming aware of one's true potential, character, motives."*
Self-discovery concerns itself with 'finding yourself' and discovering who you are. This is an essential journey to embark on — one that will help you discover your purpose in life and set you free, as brilliantly stated by Ralph Ellison: *"When I discover who I am, I'll be free."*

SENSE OF PURPOSE

This principle speaks of certainty about your path and progress in life. Knowing what you want and being definite about it, guided by a burning desire, determination, and passion. By observing this principle, you are making sure that you are not distracted or drift from your path, as discussed extensively in Chapter 3. This grants you a sense of purpose and direction in life. In these modern times, where a lot of people are purposeless, aimless and plunge into vices and issues, developing a deep sense of purpose is vital as you seek to achieve success in life. It also keeps you on the right path, and usually comes from you discovering who you are, which is your purpose in life.

PERSONAL VISION

Personal vision is the next essential pattern. A vision is a picture of your desired future from your heart. It is an internalised clear mental image of a preferred future. This is seeing the end from the beginning. Personal vision is such a vital pattern for your life. If you are going by the definition, it suggests an inner awareness or knowledge of a future that you want or like. In life, there are many potholes, so if you can see where you are going before you get there, then you are most likely to get there. No matter what unfavourable circumstance you encounter in your journey, you can turn it to your advantage, like 'turning lemons into lemonade.' I know you are asking, "If it's that important, then why is everyone not doing it?" Someone rightly said, "*Eyes that look are common; eyes that see are rare.*"

This is the principle that will take you from where you are right now in life to the future you want or desire. Vision gives birth to a mission, which is your general assignment in life. A mission requires certain steps to ensure completion. Each step accounts for a desired goal. In life, it is important to achieve your goals, complete your mission and fulfil your vision. Simply put, to get the vision fulfilled, there are necessary actions you must take, coupled with clearly-defined goals and plans - this is the highway to manifest success in life.

BELIEVE IN YOURSELF

Believing in yourself means confidence in one's self and one's abilities. You must have confidence in yourself and your abilities, knowing that what you have accomplished does not define who you are.

It is about recognising and being personally persuaded of the treasure in you and your uniqueness. As a result, you become original, authentic or simply – yourself. Belief determines expectations. If you want to succeed, focus more on your beliefs. You will experience on the outside, what you believe on the inside. This is living from the inside out. When people believe in themselves, they unleash the power in themselves and resources around them that almost immediately take them to a higher level. Belief helps you to see the picture of what is in you. You can:

- Start by believing in your potential; your untapped power or reservoir of treasures that are within you.
- Believe in your mission. Your mission is your general assignment in life; what you have committed yourself to do.
- Believe that it is possible. Believe whatever you have to do is within the limits of ability, capacity, or realisation.

FOCUS

Focus is giving special attention to something. Energy flows where attention goes, so whatever you focus your attention on becomes dominant in your life. You need to ensure that you do not let the 'distractions distract you.' By observing the principle of focus, you can be productive with your time. Achievers are people who are very focused and very productive. For young people, many things are vying for your attention. Therefore, your ability to focus on what is important to you and then go on to do them is key and will earn you great rewards in life and enable you to achieve a lot within a specified time frame.

USE YOUR IMAGINATION

Imagination is the ability to form a mental image of something that is not perceived through the five senses. The mind can build mental scenes, objects or events that do not exist, are not present, or have happened in the past.

Imagination is a creative power that is necessary for inventing an instrument, designing a dress or a house, painting a picture or writing a book. The creative power of imagination is instrumental to your success in any field. What we imagine with faith and feelings comes into being. Imagination has a great role and value in each one's life. It is much more than just idle daydreaming. We all use our imagination, whether consciously or unconsciously, in our everyday experiences.

Your imagination is your creative centre. Using your imagination to figure out solutions to existing and future problems or issues is priceless. Achievers have used their imagination to birth great inventions and technology. In the same way, using yours will put you in a position to create amazing results. Your imagination will help you to determine what is next for you when you are unsure of what to do or if you get stuck.

PERSISTENCE

During the California Gold Rush, two brothers sold their possessions and went searching for gold, otherwise known as prospecting. One day, they discovered a vein of gold shining within its ore and staked a claim to be the first one to begin mining the gold ore out of the mine. All went well at first, but then something strange happened. The vein of gold ore disappeared! They had come to the end of the rainbow, and the pot of gold was no longer there. The brothers continued to pick away, but without success. Finally, they gave up in disgust. They sold their mining equipment and claim rights for a few hundred dollars and took the train back home.

The man who purchased the claim hired an engineer to examine the rock strata of the mine. The engineer advised him to continue digging in the same spot where the former owners had left off, and three feet deeper, the new owner struck gold. A little more persistence and the two brothers would have been millionaires.

There is gold in you too. Do you need to dig three feet deeper? Persistence is the quality that allows someone to continue doing something or trying to do something even though it is difficult or opposed by other people. It is fuel to get you to your desired goal. Persistence always wins.

As Winston Churchill once said, *"success is stumbling from failure to failure with no loss of enthusiasm."*

The attitude of an Achiever is never to give up and persist until they win. Achievers do not allow the setbacks in life to derail them from their pursuit. As you work towards your dreams and goals, you will face obstacles and impediments in your life. You ought not to allow these setbacks to pull you back. Have the strength of heart and boldness and confront the issues of life and win always.

MENTORSHIP

Mentorship breeds success. It helps bring the best out of you. Bob Proctor said, *"A mentor is someone who sees more talent and ability within you than you see in yourself, and helps bring it out of you."* A mentor partners with you to reach your goal in life. John C. Maxwell said, *"One of the greatest values of mentors is their ability to see ahead what others cannot see and to help them navigate a course to their destination"*.

Achievers surround themselves with tutors and trainers. There is nothing new under the sun. The things you desire to achieve have been done before. But it is your willingness to learn from people who are ahead of you, who have done it and experienced it, that is a sign of one of the patterns of successful people.

YOUR NETWORK

Jim Rohn advises that *"you are the average of the five people you spend the most time with."* The people you spend the most time with shape who you are. They determine what conversations dominate your attention. They can influence your attitudes and behaviours. Eventually, you start to think as they think and behave as they behave. Therefore, surround yourself with the right people. Surround yourself with the dreamers and the doers, the believers and thinkers. Surround yourself with those who see greatness within you, even when you do not see it yourself!

Robert Kiyosaki stated that *"the richest people in the world look for and build networks. Everyone else looks for a job."* You are as rich as your network. It is also said that *"Your network is your net worth."* There is an obvious reason the world's most successful business leaders are also incredible at building relationships. Success in nearly every aspect of life comes down to your ability to build meaningful relationships – both personal and professional. There is a correlation between building meaningful relationships and your net worth.

An achiever takes its network seriously. You must learn to build a strategic alliance with people who will propel you, encourage you and help you to get to the next level. No man is an island, so our willingness to connect with people, respect and value relationships is priceless.

PERSONAL DEVELOPMENT

A father sits at the kitchen table, drinking a cup of coffee while reading the newspaper when his son comes running downstairs, ready to go out and play. Earlier in the week, he promised his son that they would spend the day together. Although he had blocked off the entire day to spend quality time with his son, he wanted a few more minutes to conclude his morning routine with finishing reading the newspaper. To buy himself a few more minutes, the father rips out a picture of the world in the newspaper into twenty tiny pieces, places them on the table in front of his son and tells him that as soon as he finishes the puzzle, they will go outside and play. Less than three minutes go by when his son excitedly pulls down the newspaper and says, "I'm done!" The father looks up, astonished and asks his son how he was able to complete the task so quickly. His son explained that a piece fell on the floor, and when he bent over to pick it up, he could see through the bottom of the glass table that there was a picture of a man on the back of all the little pieces. So he sat back up, turned all the pieces over and put the man together. Once he did that the world just fell into place.

This story is directly related to personal development. When our inner world is enhanced and improved, our outer world will be beautiful.

Personal development is directly connected to the individual's self-improvement. You never stop adding value to yourself because life is a journey. You must constantly be self-improving. Personal development is the idea that you are responsible for improving yourself and continuously developing. There is a Japanese philosophical concept called *'Kaizen'*, founded on the belief that everything can be improved, and nothing remains the same. While there is no direct English translation, Kaizen closely translates to *'change for the good.'* It is a compound of two Japanese words that together translate as *'good change'* or *'improvement'*, but *Kaizen* means *'constant, continuous improvement'*, and is a mindset you can apply anywhere, no matter where you are in life, and develop into becoming the achiever you were born to be.

REFLECTION

CHAPTER TEN

Time With Young Achievers

You are the average of the 5 people
you spend the most time with.
– Jim Rohn

Time With Young Achievers (TWYA) is a special programme dedicated to exploring the work of young people who are on the Path of Achievers. This programme sees the brightest side of life and brings to light young people who are making an effort to do great things and contribute meaningfully to their communities and the world at large. It attempts to correct the negative notion that most societies hold about young people. It is a celebration of Young Achievers. My definition of a young achiever is someone who has discovered themselves and is advancing towards a worthwhile goal.

At TWYA, we engage with young achievers in a conversational interview style, offering them a platform to share their story and ideas, and inspire other young people towards the Path of Achievers.

Our vision for TWYA is to create an enduring platform that will give a voice to young achievers to share their success stories with the world. We are on a mission to be the inspiring voice in this generation by building a vast network of young achievers around the world – **a network of model young leaders**. This programme will impact as many young people who are inspired to discover themselves and be the achievers they were born to be.

Young Achievers Unleashed

After more than ten years of mentoring and coaching, it is remarkable to see the multitude of young people that are doing incredible and ground-breaking things. Nevertheless, the majority of the news reports about young people is through a negative lens, which perpetuates negative stereotypes in our society. I believe this unbalanced portrayal of youth is a grave injustice. As someone who has personally witnessed the evolution of young people, I am committed to their potential and rebalancing the scales. I believe and have confidence in tomorrow's future leaders. The youth are the reason for this book; to help them understand their untapped power and ability to become young achievers now, not later in life, and see results. Young achievers are people who have discovered themselves and are advancing toward a worthwhile goal.

There are young people who are truly doing amazing things around the world.

Celebrating Young Achievers

One of the greatest habits we can develop is celebrating the achievements of others. This will attract success, and the same or similar achievements to your life. We celebrate and share the stories of the following young achievers so that their stories will inspire you.

The principle of celebrating others' achievements is a culture.

Success Stories of Young Achievers

Often, there are countless numbers of people that apply certain life principles and achieve great results. We must recognise such people and share their stories to inspire many more young people who are poised to become the people that they were born to be. These young achievers are people that have not only discovered themselves or their potential but are literally living out their seed talents or purpose on Earth. In a world that labels our youths with all kinds of negative connotations, I have come across some amazing young people and decided to include some of their stories in this book, in the hope that it will inspire others to become who they were born to be.

These are the success stories of five Young Achievers in the UK recorded at the time this book was written. I strongly believe that these ones will go on to do greater things!

Emilio's Story, 19
Emilio Gay, Professional Cricketer

I come from a multicultural background with my dad's family being from Grenada, and my mum's from both England and Italy.

By no means have I been brought up poor, but certainly not rich either. It hasn't always been easy for my parents financially supporting me through the years before getting to this level, but money isn't needed to make it professionally. All I ever needed was their support, which I've had.

My dad used to throw balls at me when I was as young as four, but I mainly learned to play football and cricket as well, side by side. This was until I went to Grenada in 2007 for the World Cup and fell in love with the game, which then made it clear to me that becoming a professional cricketer was exactly what I wanted to do. I've always had an extreme passion for the sport, which explains why I have gotten to the point I am.

Compared to the other kids I would often compete with, I didn't think I was as talented. My dedication, hard work, consistency and belief is the reason I am here today. The real turning point for me was when I didn't get into the Bunbury Festival at age 15. This was my first real exposure to playing with and against the best of the 15-year-olds in the country. When my mum told me I didn't get it, I cried. I remember it like it was yesterday. The very next day, I said to my dad, "Let's go to the nets. I'll prove them all wrong!"

I've always worked hard, but ever since then, I've trained relentlessly to get here. Day in, day out, never skipped a training session in years. Getting up at 3am to go for runs in the cold, going to the gym at 4am, going to the nets with my dad at 5am, just scoring a big century and going to the nets straight after. Studying the game in my spare time, night after night. While all my peers were spending their time partying, drinking and socialising, I was working. I got into the academy late at 17, while the other boys started at 14. I have faced many challenges up until this point. I again didn't get into the Under-17s national tournament at the age of 16. The following year I got a stress fracture in my back and was out for the whole season. I remember when my mum was telling my dad and me the news, she also said: "It doesn't mean it's the end." I started crying, thinking, *Surely it can't be the end after all that work*.

My whole life, I've had people tell me, "You're good, but there's an incredibly small chance as not that many people make it." When I joined the academy, there were 11 boys altogether, and I knew in the coaches eyes I wasn't as good as some of the others. One coach said, "You're the most talented group of academy boys, but realistically, only 1 or 2 of you will make it". I looked around and said to myself, That's *1000%* going to be me, they don't want it like I do. Most people kind of want it, they don't want it bad, it's not an obsession. They don't want it any more than they want to party, or sleep. Most people would rather sleep than work. You need to get to the point where you're willing to sacrifice sleep. Two years later, all the other ten have been released.

They didn't put in the work that I did and didn't have the self-belief I had. If you want to make it and make it big in sport, you need to be different.

It's taken me a while to realise what my why was, and I'm a firm believer that everyone needs a strong why to really succeed in life. Despite being self-motivated, my why inspires me always. What do I mean by a 'why'? Why do you get up in the morning and do what you do? You need a reason behind your work, so when you are hit with adversities, or you don't feel in the mood, your why will get you through it. My why is the sacrifice my parents have made for me. My mum for driving all over the country for me to go training and matches, spending all night helping me find sponsors for my kit – my mum is my number one supporter. My dad for throwing literally thousands and thousands of balls at me, whether it's 5am or 5pm, whether he's just got back from a long day or it's his day off, if there are three certainties in life, it's death, taxes, and my dad going to the nets with me and stopping when I'm ready to stop. How can I quit after that? How can I face adversity and not like the process and not give 110% every single day? I'm not just playing for myself. I want to put them in a financially great position when I'm older, as, without them, I wouldn't be close to where I am.

I would like to believe I have already made a positive impact on younger people despite only being 19. Some kids do look up to me as a role model, so coaching or giving them advice when I can have hopefully made a difference for them, big or small. I know what it's like to see people I look up to and for them to give me the time of day, so hopefully, when I'm older, I can make that same level of impact.

My mentors have always been my parents, to whom I go for advice as they know what's best for me. I do have a coach that I go to for technical advice, whom I trust more than any other coach, as I've done a lot of work with him over the years.

My advice to any young sportsman is this: work harder than the person on your left and the person on your right. For me, I always think to myself you may be smarter than me, you may be richer than me, you may have parents who know loads of people, but you will never outwork me. Never be outworked by anyone. Dedicate yourself, have self-discipline and be committed. Commitment isn't saying I'll do it on the day that feels good. Commitment is still doing it for 2 hours though you only planned for 1 hour. In 5 years, are you still doing the same thing? On the days you don't want to, when it's cold and wet, when you're tired or when you're in such good form you feel like you don't need to — that's commitment. Finally, believe in yourself and have a strong *why*. Sports is mainly mental. Don't let anyone tell you that you can't do something or you're not the best. Be motivated when things don't go your own way as that will happen in sport, and find your why, keep it close to you, and use it to inspire you when things get tough, and most importantly, never make excuses.

Lotanna's Story, 22
Lotanna Ezeike, Entrepreneur,
CEO of XPO & Lash Batch

Creating your own luck

I'm Lotanna Ezeike, a 22-year-old black boy from ends. I've been able to follow my dreams and create a tech company valued at £500k. Our aim is to make influencer marketing scalable for small businesses in the UK.

My background brought me here. I went to a public school that was closed down due to gang violence. I believe I learnt the most important trait there - resilience. The idea (of XPO) came from a personal issue my co-founder and I had. Influencers are difficult to work with. However, instead of complaining, we decided to get to the root of the problem.

We soon found out that the core issues were communication and payment. Influencers have no place to funnel their business enquiries and are forced to sift through hundreds of DMs/Emails they already get. Payments: brands hated paying influencers pre-post due to scams or general low trust. I've never been a complainer (as most people are). I've never believed I was owed anything. If I have a problem, I will go out there and fix it, and if it's a big enough problem people will pay to use it, right?

We had no coding background, no connection and no money. So, we decided to outsource a developer. We found one through Twitter. Soon enough, Tomi and I were working with this developer and essentially paying him monthly from my salary. In total, the project cost £10K+, and a few days before launch he disappeared. He essentially scammed us. We were back to Square 1. No coding background, no connection and NO money. I went through a depressive state for a few weeks but then thought actually to teach myself how to code. This was the best decision of my life. Luckily, a friend referred a guy called Franck he met at a networking event. I reached out over LinkedIn, and within 3-4 weeks, he was our third founder.

We went through so many ups and downs with trying to integrate Instagram API – this allows influencers to sign in with their Instagram account. Instagram eventually blocked us from using that functionality due to the whole Facebook privacy shenanigans. We eventually launched in September 2019, and our user base has been growing 30% every single week. I've learnt so much as a CEO, especially in terms of people management.

I'm hopeful for the future and looking forward to what it holds for me.

My tips for being successful in business:
1. Take every opportunity that comes your way.
2. You don't need to go to networking events if you're not actually networking.
3. Focus on improving your product based on user feedback, not on what your friend says.

Derrick's Story, 26

Derrick Osaze, Professional Boxer, Youth Pastor, Director of AIM Youth UK

My name is Derrick Osaze, and I'm 26. I am a full-time professional boxer, run my own Youth Organisation, and I am a Youth Pastor.

I am the fifth born of six children and of Nigerian descent. I was born in London, but now residing in Nottingham, where I attended Nottingham Trent University. I have two degrees: a BA (Hons) in Business Management and Master of Research (MRes) in Sports Psychology. I am happily married and have been for over two years.

How did you discover what you wanted to do/be?

I've always dreamt of becoming a boxer. I started at the age of 15, but it wasn't until I was 21, after I won my first national championship in 2015, that I really started to have more confidence in myself and my ability, believing that I could have a career in boxing. More than anything, I felt like it was where God was calling me to be. I got into boxing to keep out of trouble really. Aged 15, I had been excluded from school almost 20 times and on the verge of being permanently expelled due to my temperament. So, I turned to boxing after my friend encouraged me to give it a try. He reckoned it would be a great way to channel my energy positively. I quickly fell in love with boxing, and it went from a hobby to a passion, and now it's a lifestyle. Boxing saved my life, and I am certain that God led me to boxing. The sport has taught me so much, the biggest lesson being self-discipline. It positively shaped my character and kept me out of trouble.

What are you passionate about?

I am passionate about God and everything to do with God, being His faithful servant, carrying out His instructions, following the path He has for me which includes ministry, my family and boxing, which I am all passionate about. I believe my purpose is to help to inspire and motivate people to be better versions of themselves, helping to orchestrate change in the process. Ultimately my main purpose is to ensure God gets all the glory as it says in Colossians 3:23. My ultimate goal is to fully fulfil the purpose which God created me for and help bring glory to His name!

Where do you see yourself in 10 years?

In 10 years, I see myself living happily in a nice house with my wife and five children, numerous title belts and a games room!! Travelling as much as I can with my family to see more of the world and eating everything I can get my hands on, from cookies to hot wings. Ha, ha!! In addition to that, on a more serious note, I would just want to spend quality time with my family and make up for any lost time due to the time constraints of my career. I would want to carry on my work with young people and start a youth charity that empowers them to reach their full potential. Then at some point, I see myself going into ministry on a full-time basis.

What inspires you?

My biggest inspiration is God and ensuring that I make God proud to call me His son when it's all said and done. I would like to think that I have been impactful in the things that I do and stand for, but I believe that this is something only God and people other than myself can determine to what extent I have made an impact or not in what I do.

What's your take on mentorship?
And do you have a mentor?

I believe mentorship is very important, especially when you can find a mentor who has had a similar path and journey to one that you desire. You can gain so much wisdom, advice and expertise from their experiences. I also believe that you should not be limited to just one mentor. I have a few different mentors that cover various areas of my life such as ministry, boxing and family, that I look to for advice and guidance. Furthermore, I believe mentorship is more than just speaking to a mentor but observing what they do and learning from their actions.

What are your top tips for success?
- Always put God first in everything you do.
- Believe and Dream Big with God.
- Pray hard like you're not working and work hard like you're not praying!

Stephanie's Story, 24
Stephanie Itimi, Social Entrepreneur,
Executive Director of Seideasi

My name is Stephanie Itimi, and I'm 24 years old. I currently work full time for Essex County Council as a Senior Equality and Partnerships Advisor. I manage different partnerships with the University of Essex working on their data programme, and I also do event management. Outside of my full-time role, I have two organisations.

The first is Seideasi, which is a social enterprise, and it's all about helping Black, Asian and Ethnic Minority women enter the cyber security field, and we do this through events, recruitment events, mentorship programmes, virtual internships, as well as having a jobs board where we let them know on a monthly basis what jobs are out there. It started from 2018. Generally, I was focusing on helping women in my local area with skills such as Microsoft Excel, and just how to use a computer. Then I also have a coding club for girls, teaching girls from age 9-16 in my local area how to code. And then it grew because at that time I was working within cyber security and I saw there was a lack of diversity. Firstly, very few women were involved, and when you look at the women, very few are from a minority ethnic background. Seideasi was really trying to tackle that because a lot of the women were asking me "How can we get into the field?"

My second organisation is called Seinfo, and it's a charity located and registered in Nigeria, and that's an online platform for people to learn, and it scales from web design to building apps. The reason why I wanted to do it was because I realised that with the way the world is moving, especially with the future of work websites like PeoplePerHour and Fiverr, you don't really need that person to be in the same room as you and this has changed the whole landscape of work. Unfortunately, in a lot of African countries, there is a huge number of unemployed and the idea is if I'm able to help African women and African youth with this free platform, then we'll be able to help people to be economically independent and empowered.

The next phase, which is what I'm working on now, I'm partnering up with digital trainers in different African countries. We have someone in Burkina Faso and in Kenya and three people in Nigeria from different states (Enugu, Kaduna and Abuja). Once we have been able to raise enough donations, we can then hopefully make it into an app where people will be able to access the information at the tips of their fingers without wasting so much data.

How did you discover what you wanted to do?

I would say I was one of those kids that had loads of career changes. I first wanted to be an accountant because I wanted loads of money! Then I was really obsessed with being an engineer and that's because I watched the movie Back to the Future, I was really obsessed with robots and creating things, and in those times when they had the big TVs with the big back, I would take it apart and look behind it to see how the circuits align. So, I genuinely thought career-wise, I was going to be an electrical engineer and wanted to study it.

However, I had a rude awakening when I did my A-Level Physics and completely hated it, and failed it. I had to then pick a subject, so I picked Sociology, and what I love about it is that it tugs my heartstrings, reminding me of something that I encountered when I was 15. When I was 15, I went back to Nigeria for the first time in a very long time. I remember we went early and were there for a month and kids were still in school at this point, and my mum and I were in the car which stopped at the gas station, and I saw this young boy literally on the street selling oranges and I remember asking my mum why is this young boy not in school? And the answer was that not everyone is fortunate enough to go to school, his family can't afford it, so he has to sell. This boy was like six, and I remember thinking, *In this life I have to fight poverty. Whatever I do has to fight poverty.* And when I thought I would be an electrical engineer the plan was that I would create things that would allow people to better their lives, whether that's making things to help people with diseases or just to have tech for good. And when I did sociology, it was like, OMG, this is my subject! And the reason I say that is because it focuses on things like family: why they are the way they are; why are certain parts of society not aligned? Why are they struggling to meet up? And it really changed my perspective on a lot of things.

I think finding my true self is a process. Right now, I'm still finding myself. I think all these experiences have made me realise that I'm very passionate about empowering women and people from minority backgrounds. This includes empowering them economically through technology and skills, knowledge information, mentorship, etc. Anything I can do to empower someone to get a higher paying job or skills to upscale their business – that's what my passion is. Going back to when I was 15, where I vowed to tackle poverty, I really believe that I am doing that right now.

Where do you see yourself in 5-10 years?

Impact. I don't know where exactly Seideasi will be, but I want it to be where people learn the skills to get into jobs. In those jobs, I would like there to be unions that protect the rights of those workers in the jobs because I believe that unions are a very powerful thing especially for someone from a minority background in the UK. Long term, I see myself having that 360° outlook of empowering women all over the world, but mostly in developing and emerging markets. Also, empowering them to enter the cyber security field. I would like the impact to be that because there are more women from BAME (diverse backgrounds) that we would have policies and technologies that would protect migrant women from labour and sexual exploitation.

I hope that with Seideasi, I'm able to get more women who are from minority backgrounds within that global number. I would love that impact to translate into better-suited technology and policies to protect us. Being online is deadly, e.g., the things going on, kidnapping, etc. – it's horrendous. So that's the impact I want to have.

I want more Africans – and Africa itself – to be the hub for software engineers, graphic designers, virtual assistants, or anything to do with technology. With the way this world is going and the speed it's moving at, I don't want African youth and African women to be left behind. The hopeful prayer that I have is that people can benefit and have jobs without having to leave Nigeria.

What inspires you?

Keke Palmer inspires me because she was one of the first people I saw who was doing many things, e.g., a dancer, an actor, musician, presenter, etc., with so many talents. The fact that she's been able to manoeuvre all those talents is truly inspiring as I also have so many passions and sometimes it's hard to see how everything aligns, but she inspires me in this way.

Another person who inspires me is my mum, my dad and my family. The sacrifices they've made for me to have an education in the UK inspire me. Women also inspire me in general. The stories I hear of things they've had to overcome are very inspiring to me because with older women it makes me think, this is what I could face, and their advice is showing me how I can manoeuvre that.

How have you been impactful?

My greatest impact involves speaking at events and the things I'm involved in, as previously mentioned. The fact that this year we've already trained 216 women or that the coding club has trained 29 BAME girls really makes me happy. I know I'm meant to be doing this for money, but I'm genuinely happy that I'm able to have a positive impact on people's lives – people I care about.

What would you say are some tips for success?

Don't care about what people say. The reason I say that is, when you do things like entrepreneurship, sometimes you feel like you're going against the grain or you're different, and it can be isolating because it can feel like people don't understand the vision, but I would say keep at it. You have to motivate yourself and think about the end goal, no matter how difficult. You have to be grateful for what you have achieved, and that's what's helped me a lot.

Baran's Story, 16

Baran Korkmaz, Founder & CEO of ARWAY

I started my first venture, which was selling pirated software, at the age of 11. It was an editing software. At that time, everyone wanted to be a YouTuber, and one thing they were all missing was being able to edit videos. So, I downloaded this software from the Internet for free, and I found that I could sell it to friends and others in my school who wanted to experiment with YouTube. I had a very interesting way of selling the software: I went around to each person's house, and with a USB stick, I was able to install the software. I charged a fair price, between £20-£30, for each installation, and that was my first ever glimpse of how businesses work. I learnt about how a demand is created and how to supply that demand, and profit from it. Also, because I got the software for free, over a period of a few months, I was able to turn over a few hundred pounds in profit. This was quite a lot of money for me at that time. I then realised that this was my calling, that business was definitely something I wanted to get into.

The thing I found most interesting about tech was that you could deploy it anywhere and use it to get my product across. And to me, I think that's the real power of tech. The main reason why I did it was because I wanted to create something and be able to say it's my own product. My first venture opened the door for many more ventures like when I went on holiday in Turkey, I wanted to use the money I made from the software and invest it in handmade bracelets that I thought I would be able to sell in the UK. I brought a lot back, but in the end, it didn't really work out. And that was my first lesson, and the first failure really. When it came down to it, there was no demand for it, and it was a really bad mistake since what I did was buy the stock before seeing the demand or the market, and that taught me a lot in terms of what it means to fail.

I think failure is very key at an early stage. The advantage of starting young was that I could fail and get back up really quickly. I've had other failures as well – the bracelets weren't the only other thing. I tried to sell a computer repair service in my local area since I learnt and taught myself more about computer repairs and repaired my own computer and reinstalled the operating systems. Even for that, I printed out leaflets. I invested in setting up a Facebook page small ad campaign, and I still did not generate anything from it. So, all of those and a bunch of other small ventures I did when I was younger – all of this really contributed to teaching me the key lessons in life. Not just in life, but in business, about how to go about it.

Fast forward to 2019, what I'm doing now. It has really helped me in setting up my first tech start-up because it taught me how to work with people, how the market works, how to actually close deals, close sales. And it really gave me this personal feeling of core salesmanship, and it is something I've always carried with me, and I think I will continue to carry.

So up until now the biggest event we've had has been with Arway, the app I started. I taught myself how to code when I was 11, and since then, with all those small ventures I saw a demand initially out of a problem which was with the Grenfell disaster in the summer of 2017.

I think the biggest problem with that was that the authorities did not react quickly enough and I think all the protocols were thrown out the window. From that, I was inspired to take action and create a scalable way that actually works: being able to position people inside the building and locate them for authorities to be able to rescue them faster. So I went about creating an initial prototype. Around this time the latest software came out called ARKit and ARCore. So initially it was only ARKit, but once that came out, I started prototyping a solution where not only would authorities be able to locate users inside the building, but users would also be able to find their way out of the building and be able to navigate outside to the nearest exit.

So that was the initial prototype I took to competitions and different award shows, and I picked up a lot of attractions from there. The first one was the British invention show, The Big Bang Fair, and from there, I gained a lot of insight and actually was featured on Sky News. A reporter was looking around the British invention showroom, and they saw me with my stall, and they found out I was the youngest person there with my solution. There were all sorts of other international competitors from Malaysia, the Philippines to Saudi Arabia – people from all corners of the world and all walks of life. It was an international competition, and they really loved my solution, so I picked up two awards from that British invention show, and that really fuelled my investment and my own commitment. I saw that actually instead of just being a safety tool and just a project, I wanted to turn it into something more and that's just when it really turned into a start-up I wanted to do.

At this time, I picked up a few business books. I really wanted to learn how I could position myself as a founder, and so my journey had really started back when I was 14. Once I started educating myself in the world of start-ups, I was learning more and more. I picked up a lot of key skills, and that's actually when I realised I couldn't do everything on my own.

Coincidentally, just after winning the British invention award, I heard from Dovydas, (later to be my co-founder), after posting on Twitter. Initially, he just congratulated me on my work, on the Sky News feature. By that time, I was thinking about turning it into something bigger, bigger than just a once-off project. I wanted to actually make this something that was installed and implemented everywhere. So Dovydas reached out on Twitter, and I responded saying, "I see that you are a software developer. Is there any chance this is something you would like to work on as well?"

That's where the compensation started. I had no idea what I was doing, how to form a team or anything like that. But I found there were software developers out there, and this whole community was really open online, so the key lesson I picked up there is shoot your shot. Don't be afraid to connect with someone.

Fast forward to the moment I started working with Dovydas. We created a lot of good prototypes, the platform solution. However, we wanted to make something that was actually sellable and actually worked in the market. And what happened was we started our first test on the market by trying to set up some pilots, and by that time, I was also introduced to our other co-founder who is based in India. His name is Nickel, and he is our Chief Product Officer. He helped us shaped the core architecture of the system and really helped us to get to where we are today with the first project being in the HCG Hospital (Largest cancer care network in South Asia), where we had a way of finding solutions for the healthcare, and from there we were able to demonstrate how useful this solution was for patients and visitors.

We found that there is actually a demand for this kind of solution. Going back to when I first started, with any business, the *demand* has always been the key factor that for me determines whether it is something I would like to pursue and whether it actually has the potential.

From that, it really catapulted us forward with setting up some more projects and actually working with the largest VR company in Qatar to set up a custom solution for their space, and now with their most recent client, working in the world's largest shopping mall in Taiwan, Dream Mall.

We have also received an acquisition offer for the business to join a much larger company in expanding their product or frame completely.

Throughout this journey, it has really been insightful for me to grow as a person, and I have always kept that determination about myself where if I want to achieve something, I'm going to achieve it. I think that's all: perseverance. And that's key in any start-up and in anything since at the very early stages you don't often see much (in terms of results, profits, etc.), and we were always focused on the bigger picture.

Of course, when times get rough, you look down on it, but we always kept it above ourselves to focus on that. Up until now, we have the acquisition offer, working with these current clients that we have, and we are always getting new requests, and we have a lot of advanced leads set up for 2020.

So, we are really excited to make Arway a success and plan to demonstrate it online since we haven't revealed too much yet, but we really hope to make an impact with what we are doing. Right now we still see it as the beginning, since the offer we received was in 7 figures. That's a key indicator that we are on the right track and we hope to continue on this track and grow from it and make the most out of it, so really that's my story.

I'm now 16, living in London, currently working on Arway full time. After completing my GCSEs, I had offers to continue my education. However, I decided to pursue my passion rather than take the conventional education route. I will just continue working in the tech industry, finding tech solutions for problems, continue to grow myself in the industry and eventually become a leader. My biggest goal is to use tech to push the human race forward and leave a legacy behind. Ten years from now, I will continue to work in tech, finding solutions, but on a larger scale, while exploring different industries and opportunities, I hope to add value and solve problems.

I believe mentoring is key for personal development and growth of a young and new entrepreneur. There are three types of mentors you should have/be:

1. Be a mentee of someone who is one level above you; this could be a CEO in the industry you aspire to work in.

2. Connect with someone who is on the same level/position as you to share ideas and talk.

3. Give back by mentoring others and learning more yourself through your own teachings. I have a mentor, a CEO friend and someone whom I mentor. These three key people help in my own self-improvement as I continue on this journey.

My top tips for success are: uncertainty is expected at any stage – even if you run the largest company in the world or you're just starting out, you will always have a shadow of uncertainty in what you do, whether that's not knowing that you'll make ends meet for your business or considering to drop out, you need to embrace the uncertainty in your actions and accept the risk of being a trailblazer off the well-worn path. Even if you're wrong and it does not work out, the advantage of being young will always give you unlimited tries that make it easy for you to pick it up again.

YOUNG ACHIEVERS GROUP (YAG)

Become an achiever today! Join the Young Achievers Group and start writing your success story!

About Us

Young Achievers Group is a social enterprise focused on helping young people to decide on their career paths by mentoring and coaching them to discover their talents and gifts, enabling them to impact their generation.

YAG was born out of the idea that every young person can make a difference in their world if and when they encounter the right ideas and principles. We encourage young people to be responsible for their own lives.

Our vision is building a network of model young leaders around the world.

We are on a mission to inspire young people to discover their seed-talents.

We are motivated by seeing young people discover a deeper meaning for their lives.

We believe that everyone was born with a seed-talent, and that self-discovery is the key to self-manifestation, and we believe (and put into practise) the concept of living from the inside out.

We offer a wide range of services, including mentorship and coaching. Contact us to sign up for our mentorship and coaching programmes.

The Young Achievers Group designs and delivers quality, proven programmes to empower young people to become responsible, productive and significant adults and to contribute significantly to their communities and the world at large.

Visit our website to find out more!
www.youngachieversgroup.com

REFLECTION

Conclusion

An achiever is someone who has discovered themselves and is advancing towards a worthwhile goal. An achiever looks within to find an innate reason for living. They know that the answer is within and not without. Over a century ago, Russell Conwell echoed the overarching lesson in this book in his lecture series *'Acres of Diamonds.'* At the heart of *'Acres of Diamonds'* was a parable Conwell heard while travelling through present-day Iraq in 1870, and in summary, it goes like this:

There was once a wealthy man named Ali Hafed who lived not far from the River Indus. He was content because he was wealthy and wealthy because he was content. One day a priest visited Ali and told him about diamonds.

Ali heard all about diamonds, how much they were worth, and went to his bed that night a poor man. He had not lost anything, but he was poor because he was discontented and discontented because he feared he was poor.

Ali sold his farm, left his family, and travelled to Palestine and then to Europe searching for diamonds. He did not find them. His health and his wealth failed him. Dejected, he cast himself into the sea.

One day, the man who had purchased Ali's farm was watering his animals in the stream that ran through the property and noticed a glint in the wet sands. As he looked, he found a curious sparkling stone in a stream that cut through his land. It was a diamond. In fact, digging produced more diamonds – acres of diamonds.

This, according to the parable, was the discovery of the famed diamonds of Golconda. It was one of the richest diamond finds in history; the mines of Golconda would yield not just a few but acres of diamonds.

This story reflects the ideas we have been discussing in this book. As brilliantly noted by Ralph Waldo Emerson, *"What lies behind us and what lies before us are tiny matters compared to what lies within us."* In other words, instead of looking ahead of you or behind you, look within you to discover your acres of diamonds. What lies inside of you is yours for the discovering. Look inside you to discover the acres of diamonds within you.

The awareness of the inward life will start you on a good footing to be responsible for your own life. You will realise that your life is in your hands and not in the hands of anybody, including your parents, teachers, and society!

In life, there are milestones that we all need to recognise. Life is a journey, a journey that you need to direct and plan consciously. The real life of man is the *'inward life'*. This book sought to bring out of you that inward life.

A life of success and fulfilment can only be reached when it is lived from the inside out. Everything that has happened in your life and that will ever happen, has its source from within you.

The environment you create within you is the environment that manifests outside. Life is truly lived when it is lived from within. The true journey in life is a journey within. This is the kind of life that touches others, makes an impact, draws things to you and puts you in the right direction.

For anyone, at any age, if you will apply these timeless principles I have shown, you will get amazing results in life. You have the power to fulfil and accomplish your mission in life. You have personal power inside of you. You can be anything you want to be, do anything you want to do, go anywhere you want to go, and nothing can stop you from being what you were born to be and to do. You can shape your environment and shape your life with these ideas you discovered in this book. Go live your best life and become the person that you were born to be.

Thank you for being on this journey with me. I trust that by now, you know and understand the principle of living from the inside out and the importance of being yourself and living authentically. Life is a journey, and it has to be one that is exhilarating, exciting and great.

RESOURCE PAGE

PERSONAL MISSION STATEMENT:
Part 1: Expressing Your Unique & Specific S-H-A-P-E

Special Gifts:

Heart (Passions, Desires):

Abilities (Talents):

Personality (Temperament):

Experiences (Skills, Education, Mistakes):

Part 2: Values

Part 3: Character Traits

To be **acquired:**

To be **discarded:**

Part 4: Role, Goals & What Will People Say? / The Legacy You Will Leave

Family:

Work:

Organisation:

Friends:

Community:

(*Insert number of years*)
PERSONAL DEVELOPMENT PLAN

Name:

Current age:

Age at (insert expiry year):

What areas of my life do I want to include? (These will be the major categories).

1.

2.

3.

My Purpose: _____

My Vision: _____

My Mission: _____

Goals for Year 1:

1.

2.

3.

Year 1 – 20XX

Categories	Goals	Actions	Comments
i.e., Financial	1. To have £15,000 in investments by 2025.	1. Open a stocks & shares ISA account. 2. Set up a weekly standing order of £50.	

PERSONAL VISION STATEMENT

Here's a template of a concluding statement that can be adapted:

I live each day observing values such as [*insert values*]. I feel energised and stirred up when [*insert passions*]. I believe in serving people in these areas [*insert purpose*].

PERSONALITY TEST

The Myers Briggs Type Indicator (MBTI) –
https://www.myersbriggs.org/home.htm?bhcp=1

The Enneagram –
https://www.truity.com/test/enneagram-personality-test-v7.6?utm_expid=.k7kFjC9OQ-ilBMcMJP0_Yw.1&utm_referrer=https%3A%2F%2Fwww.google.co.uk%2F

Clifton Strength –
https://www.gallup.com/cliftonstrengths/en/252137/home.aspx

NOTES

NOTES

NOTES

NOTES

NOTES

NOTES

NOTES

NOTES

Bibliography

Introduction

• "Day of Affirmation, University of Cape Town, South Africa. June 6, 1966", Robert F. Kennedy Memorial. Retrieved 11/9/07.

• Robert J. Kriegel and Louis Patler, If It Ain't Broke . . . Break It! (New York: Warner Books, 1991), 1.

• Dreyfus A. Edward. Living Life from the Inside Out. CreateSpace independent published 2011.

Chapter One

• "passion." Merriam-Webster Online Dictionary, 2008. Merriam- Webster Online. 17 May 2008. < http://www. merriam-webster.com/dictionary/passion>.

• Ziglar, Zig; Ziglar, Tom (2012). *Born to Win: Find Your Success Code.* Dallas: SUCCESS Media. ISBN 9780983156512.

• https://www.independent.co.uk/arts-entertainment/ music/news/travis-scott-astroworld-stampede-fans-hospital-injured-houston-a9197051.html

Chapter Two

• "emancipation"   ^ "The Emancipation Proclamation". Transcription. U.S. National Archives. January 1, 1863.

• Churchill, Winston. "Never Surrender." House of Commons, United Kingdom. 6 Jun 1940

• Alfred Nobel"   "http://history1900s.about.com/od/ medicaladvancesissues/a/nobelhistory.htm

- Coelho, Paulo. The Alchemist. San Francisco: Harper San Francisco, 1998. Print.
- https://en.wikipedia.org/wiki/The_Alchemist_(novel)
- *Cowles, Gregory (October 8, 2009). "Inside the List". The New York Times. Retrieved January 28, 2012.*

Chapter Three
- https://betterlifecoachingblog.com/2013/07/19/panning-for-gold-a-story-about-finding-your-purpose-in-life/
- Warren, Rick. The Purpose-Driven Life: What on Earth Am I Here for? Grand Rapids, Mich: Zondervan, 2002.
- Buckingham, Marcus., and Donald O. Clifton. *Now, Discover Your Strengths.* New York: Free Press, 2001.
- Buckingham, Marcus. Go Put Your Strengths to Work. New York: Free Press, 2007

Chaptet Four
- Glenn Jamie. Walk Tall, You're a Daughter of God. Deseret Book Company, 1994

Chapter Five
- https://www.psychologytoday.com/gb/blog/what-doesnt-kill-us/201608/7-qualities-truly-authentic-people

Chapter Six
- "intellect" http://dictionary.cambridge.org/dictionary/british/intellect
- "knowledge" M. Littleton, Moody Monthly, June 1989, p. 29. (http://access-jesus.com/Illustrations/Thirst-For-Wisdom)_

- Hill, Napoleon (1937). Think and Grow Rich. Chicago, Illinois: Combined Registry Company. ISBN 1-60506-930-2.
- "Joan" Marina Warner, Joan of Arc, Image of Female heroism,
- McGonigal, K. (2012). The willpower instinct: How self-control works, why it matters, and what you can do to get more of it. Avery/Penguin Group USA.
- Goleman, D. (1995). Emotional intelligence. Bantam Books, Inc.
- M. Littleton, Moody Monthly, June 1989

Chapter Seven
- McGonigal, K. (2012). The willpower instinct: How self-control works, why it matters, and what you can do to get more of it. Avery/Penguin Group USA.

Chapter Eight
- https://corporate.marksandspencer.com/documents/reports-results-and-publications/autopilot-britain-whitepaper.pdf
- Peale, Norman V. *The Power of Positive Thinking.* Englewood Cliffs, N.J: Prentice-Hall, 1956. Print.

Chapter Nine
- Sinek, Simon. Start with Why: How Great Leaders Inspire Everyone to Take Action. New York, N.Y.: Portfolio, 2009.

Conclusion
- Conwell, Russell H. Acres of Diamonds: Russell Conwell's Inspiring Classic About Opportunity. Kansas City, Mo.: Hallmark Editions, 1968. Print